BENEATH THE SURFACE

Where Old and New Testament Meet in Living Parables

"It is the glory of God to conceal a thing: but the honour of kings is to search out a matter." Proverbs 25:2

David Puffer Th.B.

WestBow
PRESS

WestBow Press books may be ordered through booksellers or by contacting:

WestBow Press
A Division of Thomas Nelson
1663 Liberty Drive
Bloomington, IN 47403
www.westbowpress.com
1-(866) 928-1240

ISBN: 978-1-4497-0125-3 (sc)
ISBN: 978-1-4497-0127-7 (hc)
ISBN: 978-1-4497-0126-0 (e)

Library of Congress Control Number: 2010924694

Illustrations by Gustave Dore

Printed in the United States of America

WestBow Press rev. date: 4/26/2010

Dedication

This book is dedicated to all those truth-seekers who are not afraid to pull back the veil of traditional interpretation and delight in what God has hidden there to His Glory.

Table of Contents

Preface

All scripture is given by inspiration of God, and is profitable for doctrine, for reproof, for correction, for instruction in righteousness: 2 Tim 3:16

The Bible is much more than history and moral instruction. It is a God-inspired document that is given to us to guide us into fellowship with our Creator. Its purpose is to lead us from the darkness of a fallen world into the light of the knowledge of a holy God.

In **1 Cor 10:11** the apostle Paul writes, *"Now all these things happened unto them for ensamples: and they are written for our admonition, upon whom the ends of the world are come."*

What things do you suppose the apostle was talking about? He was talking about the things recorded in the Old Testament. They are recorded there for our instruction and our encouragement. I call them living parables; "parables" because they represent divine instruction unto righteousness, and "living" because they are historical events and conditions that happened to real people. Also the spiritual principles contained within the Scriptures are timeless; they are as pertinent today as they were for the time and people about which they were recorded.

Looking into the Scriptures is not unlike looking into a pool of water. On the surface you will see a reflection of yourself and your surroundings. But if you look deeper you may see the image of the Savior and His mission. In this humble book, I attempt to show a glimpse of the "wheels within wheels" of divine "reveal-ation."

Introduction

My interest in the Bible did not begin until about my 40th year. I was born in Australia where beer and rugby were the predominant religions. My early years were relatively unchurched although I did believe in God. By the age of fourteen, however, I began to ask questions about Him but was completely unsatisfied with the anemic answers I got from the Christians and even ministers that claimed to know Him.

Still hungry for answers to life's mysteries, I turned to science and philosophy. These satisfied my intellect but did nothing to calm my restless spirit. I had all but given up on finding God until I met a woman at a party for the motor cycle club that I belonged to.

It was New Year's Eve 1967 and the woman was the host and the mother of one of the other members of the club. I was 23 and the 52 year old woman soon got my interest as she spoke about otherworldly things such as psychic phenomena and mystical experiences. As it turned out, she was a member of a New Age organization known as the Rosicrucian Society. I was fascinated by what she was telling me and so began my intense study of all things mystical.

I was so hungry for knowledge that I would travel hundreds of miles to learn from mediums and psychics and mystics of all kinds. I devoured books written by the great masters and I was sure that I was learning the secrets of life and discovering the mysteries of the universe.

I thought that my search for the meaning of life had finally ended but there remained a vague but powerful pull, like another voice, calling me. As I continued in my New Age studies and practices, I disregarded this inner call until one sunny day in Florida when I stood in the middle of my living room and confessed to Jesus that I did not know Him.

I was about 36 years of age and was an accomplished student of all things mystical. My New Age world view had begun to crumble however as my life took an unexpected turn and I began to have one accident after another with both cars and motorcycles. I was becoming painfully aware that I was not in control and all my great learning was of no help to me.

The still small voice that had been calling to me for so many years finally had my attention and I told Jesus, on that sunny afternoon that I would give Him a year of my life to learn from Him.

From that moment I began to read the Bible and listen to Bible tapes as intensely as I had taken to New Age so many years before. I was desperate for truth and after all the time I spent looking for it in the wrong places, somehow I knew that Jesus was the right way to it.

Within a month I was baptized and soon after that I had my first encounter with God when I clearly heard Him say to me, "What you have spent your whole life looking for, you have found in Me; welcome home."

I thought that in New Age I had found purpose and the meaning of everything but after knowing the truth that is found only in Christ, I can speak with considerable authority that New Age philosophies and all other pretenders to the truth will leave a genuine seeker hollow and disappointed.

So now, after almost 30 years of learning from Him, it is my pleasure to share a little of what He has graciously made known to me through an in-depth study of His Word and a fervent seeking of His face.

There have been many good books written to validate the message of the Bible and to defend the Christian faith; so why this one?

First of all, and perhaps most importantly, this book is not about the practical application of Christian principles to enhance the life of the believer; there are already enough of those to meet the need. Rather it is written to help the believer to see God in His glory by looking at the spiritual meaning that He has placed within the historical events recorded in the Bible.

The purpose of this book is to move the reader beyond the historicity and morality of the Word of God, as important as those are, and to show that the Bible is a truly supernatural document without equal in the sacred texts of the world's religions.

Within the pages of the Bible God has placed pictures of the promise that He made to Adam in Eden. This is the Gospel, the good news that a Savior would come and restore to man what the Devil had stolen from him.

The God revealed in the Bible is kind and beautiful and glorious beyond our understanding. And although He is infinite and transcends all human knowledge He makes Himself available to any who will seek Him with all their heart. He desires relationship with us and has provided us with everything needed to fulfill that desire.

Hear Jesus now as He invites, *"Come unto me, all ye that labour and are heavy laden, and I will give you rest. Take my yoke upon you, and learn of me; for I am meek and lowly in heart: and ye shall find rest unto your souls; for my yoke is easy, and my burden is light."* **Matthew 11:28-30**

Chapter 1

THE CREATION

As God's story begins in eternity past, man's story begins in a garden in a place called Eden (see Gen 2:8). But before Eden or the garden that God placed in it, there was the creation of the Earth.

Now, I'm not going to get involved in the battle over the age of the Earth as has become so popular among so many today. I don't know whether it is an old Earth or a young one and I find a great deal of speculation and presupposition fueling each viewpoint.

Quite frankly, after examining the evidence presented by both sides of the argument, I can truthfully say that I find nothing conclusive in either position to justify making a doctrine of it or dividing over it. In short, I don't think it matters very much how old the Earth is since its age in no way threatens the position of God as its Creator.

Whether the Earth is billions of years old or just a few millennia, I believe that all life has only been here for about six thousand years. When Archbishop James Usher, in the 17th century, traced the genealogy of the Bible back to Adam, he not only established the time of Adam's creation, but that of all life on the Earth.

The Genesis record tells us that God created plant life on the third day and that He brought light from the sun on the fourth day. This, as well as the use of the Hebrew word for "day", establishes the length of the Genesis day as a period of 24 hours, or one rotation of the Earth on its axis.

We can be sure that a day in the Genesis account was not of an unspecified length because God created plants on the third day, according to the record, and plants need sunlight in order to synthesize chlorophyll. I don't know how long a plant can live without sunlight, but I'm sure that it isn't very long.

So the Lord created vegetation on the third day and gave light from the sun on the fourth day. We can debate until the proverbial cows come home about the source of the light on the first day but whatever it was in the natural pales in significance to what it means in the spiritual.

There is, in the first chapter of the Gospel of John, a correspondence with the first few verses of Genesis that will become apparent to all but the most intransigent literalists as they are read and compared. Read them for yourself. Read them with new understanding:

John 1:1-13
In the beginning was the Word, and the Word was with God, and the Word was God.

The same was in the beginning with God.

All things were made by him; and without him was not any thing made that was made.

In him was life; and the life was the light of men.

And the light shineth in darkness; and the darkness comprehended it not.

There was a man sent from God, whose name was John.

The same came for a witness, to bear witness of the Light, that all men through him might believe.

He was not that Light, but was sent to bear witness of that Light.

That was the true Light, which lighteth every man that cometh into the world.

He was in the world, and the world was made by him, and the world knew him not.

He came unto his own, and his own received him not.

But as many as received him, to them gave he power to become the sons of God, even to them that believe on his name:

Which were born, not of blood, nor of the will of the flesh, nor of the will of man, but of God.

Now compare what you just read with the first few verses of the Bible:

Genesis 1:1-4

In the beginning God created the heaven and the earth.

And the earth was without form, and void; and darkness was upon the face of the deep. And the Spirit of God moved upon the face of the waters.

And God said, Let there be light: and there was light.

And God saw the light, that it was good: and God divided the light from the darkness.

I believe that when God penned the words of Genesis 1 He had more in mind than a lesson in astronomy or geography. See how personal those words become when seen from a spiritual viewpoint:

I submit that in the beginning we are all "without form and void". Vanity of vanities, I was an empty vessel without hope and whose end was only to be reunited with the Earth from which I was made. But God's Holy Spirit brooded over the darkness of my soul until I responded to His loving call. And He said, "Let there be light!". Then the light of the knowledge of God and the glory of His purpose flooded my soul and I became a new creature with a value and purpose that can only come from my Creator.

The Genesis record continues: On the fifth and the sixth days God filled the seas with marine life and the land with the air breathers; ALL the air breathers. This includes the dinosaurs as well as all the other animals and creeping things. Day six was also the time of God's greatest creation: Adam, the creature that was to uniquely partake of the divine nature of God. (see 2 Peter 1:4)

What an amazing destiny God has purposed for man. By choosing to follow God's leading, man is destined to resolve the Angelic conflict and restore order to God's Creation. But the enemy, Satan, continues to oppose the will of God and seeks to corrupt and destroy all that God has gloriously created.

Chapter 2

THE GARDEN IN EDEN

It is generally thought that the verses describing the garden in Eden refer to its geographic location. However, no attempt to locate such a place on the surface of the earth has been successful. Perhaps God had something other than a map for the archeologist in mind. Incidentally, as I have already pointed out, Eden is not the name of the garden. Genesis 2:8 makes it clear that God put the garden in a *place* called Eden.

In Genesis 2:9 we see that the LORD caused EVERY tree to grow out of the soil - both the Tree of Life and the Tree of the Knowledge of Good and Evil. These trees, whether real or metaphorical, present the concept of "choice".

Throughout the Scriptures God calls us to make choices. There are naturally choices that result in good and choices that result in evil. When it is noticed that the word for Eden literally means "pleasure" or "delight" and the word for garden literally means "to protect or defend", it becomes possible that the Garden in Eden is a statement concerning choice and its consequences.

Man is motivated by pleasure but there are many different ways to achieve it. Genesis 2:10 declares that out of Eden flowed a stream (the meaning of word for "stream" includes "prosperity" and "sea") that existed in four rulers, or principles, and was separated from Eden (pleasure) which was its source. If we would look at the meanings of the original Hebrew words and the roots that they are derived from, the following verses might tell us something interesting about those four principles or rulers.

The first is called Pishon, which means "to spread or disperse." The second is called Gihon, which means "to bring forth." The third is called Hiddekel which, according to Jones Book Of Old Testament Proper Names, means "swift".[1] The fourth is called Euphrates, which means "fruitfulness".

Are these speaking of principles that issue forth out of pleasure? Are these principles that, when followed, lead back to pleasure as God defines it? Could God be telling us that generosity will multiply and will swiftly bring forth fruitfulness? Surely these are principles of God's character and 2 Peter 1:4 assures us that God desires that we become partakers of His divine nature.

It is interesting that generosity and concern for others seems to be the same idea that God is presenting to us in Isaiah chapter 58. It is only in that chapter that God defines what He means by fasting, in opposition to man's ceremonial version:

Isaiah 58:6-11

Is not this the fast that I have chosen? to loose the bands of wickedness, to undo the heavy burdens, and to let the oppressed go free, and that ye break every yoke?

Is it not to deal thy bread to the hungry, and that thou bring the poor that are cast out to thy house? when thou seest the naked, that thou cover him; and that thou hide not thyself from thine own flesh? [That you provide for the need of another even at your own expense.]

---

1 Jones' Dictionary Of Old Testament Proper Names Page 153

Then shall thy light break forth as the morning, and thine health shall spring forth speedily: and thy righteousness shall go before thee; the glory of the LORD shall be thy reward.

Then shalt thou call, and the LORD shall answer; thou shalt cry, and he shall say, Here I am. If thou take away from the midst of thee the yoke, the putting forth of the finger, and speaking vanity;

And if thou draw out thy soul to the hungry, and satisfy the afflicted soul; then shall thy light rise in obscurity, and thy darkness be as the noonday:

And the LORD shall guide thee continually, and satisfy thy soul in drought, and make fat thy bones: and thou shalt be like a watered garden, and like a spring of water, whose waters fail not."

I believe that these verses are speaking of the same principles that metaphorically flow out of Eden. True pleasure is found in emulating divine character. ***God is far more pleased when we meet a need than when we perform a deed.***

The Garden in Eden was the residing place of Adam while he was in the Will of God. But when he sought his pleasure apart from the Will of God, he lost intimacy with Him and was expelled from the protected area. This separation from righteousness began a downward spiral into perversion and decay eventually leading to death.

The principle of emulating God's character holds true for Adam's offspring. We can continue to live apart from God, seeking pleasure in unrighteousness, or we can re-enter the "Garden" and partake of the Tree of Life simply by becoming transformed by the Word of God into a people suitable to fellowship with Him. In this way we begin to seek pleasure in accordance with His Holy Will.

Perhaps this is the message of the last verse of chapter three of Genesis. The cherubim are protectors of the Holiness of God. And they guard the entrance to the Garden with a flaming sword. To enter the Garden and reach the Tree of Life, the believer must be willing to be reshaped by the Word of God which is the Sword of the Spirit spoken of in Ephesians 6:17 and Hebrews 4:12.

Whether the Garden in Eden is describing a place or a condition, it definitely concerns choice. It is to be understood that God is not responsible for all of man's choices. Our choices are an integral part of the proving process of spiritual growth. God placed two trees in the Garden and offered us a choice. That choice remains with us today.

We can view life and the world either through human experience or through divine wisdom. To the believer, the Tree of the knowledge of Good and Evil is, in fact, a furnace of refinement. That is, our choices provide a measurement of spiritual growth and purity.

In Deut 30:19 God says, *"I call heaven and earth to record this day against you, that I have set before you life and death, blessing and cursing: therefore choose life, that both thou and thy seed may live …"*

Chapter 3

ENTROPY

James 1:13-15

Let no man say when he is tempted, I am tempted of God: for God cannot be tempted with evil, neither tempteth he any man:

But every man is tempted, when he is drawn away of his own lust, and enticed.

Then when lust hath conceived, it bringeth forth sin: and sin, when it is finished, bringeth forth death.

What is this death James speaks of in this passage? And where did it come from? Why is there death?

Several years ago I was watching a videotape based on the book by the astrophysicist Stephen Hawking called, "A Brief History Of Time." During one of the scenes I received what may have been a realization from the Lord regarding the truth about this mystery we call time.

It involves a word known to all scientists: Entropy. It is a word that evokes in them a response of wonder and excitement, frustration and mystery. And it is the meaning of the final word in 1 Cor 15:34: *"Awake to righteousness, and sin not; for some have not the knowledge of God: I speak this to your **shame**."*

The word "shame", in this verse, is translated from the Greek word ENTROPE, (entrope – Strongs #1791 - from the root 1788; confusion – shame). Entropy, the English version of the word. The dictionary defines it as:

en•tro•py [2]

    1 : *a measure of the unavailable energy in a closed thermodynamic system that is also usu. considered to be a measure of the system's disorder and that is a property of the system's state and is related to it in such a manner that a reversible change in heat in the system produces a change in the measure which varies directly with the heat change and inversely with the absolute temperature at which the change takes place; broadly : the degree of disorder or uncertainty in a system*

    2 a : *the degradation of the matter and energy in the universe to an ultimate state of inert uniformity*

    b : *a process of degradation or running down or a trend to disorder*

    3 : *chaos, disorganization, randomness*

All of this is just a fancy way of saying, "all things in this universe are subject to decay, disorder and death."

Entropy is widely considered to be a technical scientific term and yet it is, in fact, a Biblical word that relates to the very cause of decay and death in the physical universe. Again, "entropy" is from a Greek word that means "shame" or "confusion" and it is a compound of two Greek roots that literally means "to turn within."

---

2 Merriam Webster c1996

To the scientist, Entropy is an inescapable law of matter and energy. But there is a much deeper meaning that is known only to the spiritually aware.

You see, in this fallen universe what we call time is actually event flow; and it is stubbornly connected to decay and death. But the Word of God tells us that there was a time when there was no such thing as entropy: A time when there was neither decay nor death.

The Bible tells us that God created the Earth and the Heavens and they were perfect, without entropy. Then God created everything that is on the Earth in six days. On the sixth day He created Adam and his wife Eve.

In Genesis 2:25 we learn that they were both naked (aram 6191: bare, exposed) and were not ashamed (buwsh 954: put to shame; confused).

It is easy to assume that the nakedness of Adam and Eve was nudity, but that traditional interpretation might well be based on a Victorian sense of morality rather than on a good hermeneutic.

The meaning of the Hebrew words in this passage show us that the nakedness of Adam and Eve might be referring to the nakedness of a conscience exposed completely to an all-knowing God.

I submit that when God looked into Adam's soul He saw a reflection of Himself because Adam looked to God for all knowledge and experience. As long as Adam was a reflection of the divine nature of God, he was connected to the source of all life and without shame.

Again notice that the Hebrew word "buwsh", translated here as "ashamed", has the very same meaning as the New Testament Greek word "entrope." Both words mean "shame" or "confusion."

Simply put, while Adam and Eve were in agreement with their Creator they were innocent and unashamed. But they didn't stay that way. The Scriptures tell us that something caused them to become confused and embarrassed; to be ashamed. We discover the cause of their shame in the following verse.

Genesis 3:1
"Now the serpent was more cunning than any beast of the field which the LORD God had made. And he said to the woman, "Has God indeed said, 'You shall not eat of every tree of the garden'?"

The word *"serpent"* is translated from the Hebrew word "nachash" which derives from a root meaning, "to learn by experience." The serpent won Eve's confidence and she took the serpent's advice and looked to human knowledge and experience rather than divine guidance for truth. Her husband followed her in her folly.

It is interesting to note that the word "nachash", translated here as *"serpent"*, appears also in Genesis 30:27 where it is translated as, *"learned by experience"*: *"And Laban said unto him, I pray thee, if I have found favour in thine eyes, tarry: for I have learned by experience* (nachash) *that the LORD hath blessed me for thy sake."*

Now, Adam partook of the fruit of the tree of the knowledge of good and evil even though the LORD God had commanded him not to.

Genesis 2:16-17
"Of every tree of the garden you may freely eat; but of the tree of the knowledge of good and evil you shall not eat, for in the day that you eat of it you shall surely die."

They already had access to the Tree of Life. But they chose to partake of the Tree of the Knowledge of Good and Evil; to equate truth with their own experience.

Suddenly their carnal eyes were opened and they became spiritually blind. This was the falling away from the presence of God.

Cut off from wisdom and truth, they stumbled around with their confused minds completely exposed to the One they had turned their backs on. In their pain and embarrassment, they covered themselves with the fig leaves of their own morality; which is the only thing left when divine wisdom is lost.

Expelled from the Garden and the Tree of Life, Adam and his children could only live out their finite lives relying on their own strength and ability.

God had created a perfect universe; a perpetual habitation, life in abundance without decay or death and given it all to Adam to have dominion over. But Adam had chosen to cut himself off from the very source of life, God, and to go his own way.

In preferring his own way above that of God, Adam brought shame (entropy) into the universe. The curse of decay and death is the tragic result of separation from God who is the source of life. But even though Adam had brought the curse of entropy on the world, our gracious God announced that He would repair the damage and restore us to our original uncorrupted state.

In **Genesis 3:15** God promised that the Serpent, the lord of death and decay, would be defeated by the seed of the woman. This promise began a glorious highway of prophesy that carried the Savior of the world and the Lord of the universe from the garden in Eden to a garden called Gethsemane.

It was in Gethsemane that Jesus, the second Adam, chose to listen to the voice of his Father, and in a glorious reversal he, as our substitute, placed divine will above human will. There, in that second garden, the Devil was ignored and human attention was restored to God by the most marvelous man to ever visit this world.

It is only because of Jesus that we can come with confidence to God's throne of Grace. No longer clothed in the fig leaves of human effort and human morality but clothed in the righteousness of the Lamb of God.

Adam's shame, entropy, has been replaced by Christ's Glory and death has been swallowed up in Christ's victory. (1Cor 15:54) Praise His Holy Name forever.

A Brief Statement On The Nature Of Time

If we define time as event flow, that is, if we say that yesterday precedes today and tomorrow follows today, then we must conclude that eternity, as it is presented in the Scriptures, is an extension of that element.

However, there is a significant difference between time in eternity and time in the natural universe. As previously stated, time as event flow in this fallen universe, is stubbornly connected to decay and death.

The reason for this is simply that when Adam turned away from God, he cut the universe (which was given to him to have dominion over) off from the sustaining power of its Creator. Ever since then the universe and everything in it is moving from order to disorder, from life to death.

The Scriptures promise that this diseased universe will pass away and that God will replace it with a new and perfect universe where there will be no entropy and time as we know it will give way to an incorruptible eternity.

Chapter 4

REMOVING THE SHOES

Exodus 3:1-5

"Now Moses kept the flock of Jethro his father in law, the priest of Midian: and he led the flock to the backside of the desert, and came to the mountain of God, even to Horeb.

And the angel of the LORD appeared unto him in a flame of fire out of the midst of a bush: and he looked, and, behold, the bush burned with fire, and the bush was not consumed.

And Moses said, I will now turn aside, and see this great sight, why the bush is not burnt.

And when the LORD saw that he turned aside to see, God called unto him out of the midst of the bush, and said, Moses, Moses.

And he said, Here am I. And he said, Draw not nigh hither: put off thy shoes from off thy feet, for the place whereon thou standest is holy ground."

The Lord God said to Moses, "Remove your shoes; the place you are standing in is Holy. Come no nearer; take off your shoes." Have you ever wondered what the significance of this command was? I have.

May I share with you some of what the Lord has graciously revealed regarding the significance of the shoe in this incidence?

It is common knowledge that among the ancients the shoe was used as an instrument of property ownership. So it was considered that the ground was owned by the one who trod on it.

Deut 11:24
"Every place whereon the soles of your feet shall tread shall be yours: from the wilderness and Lebanon, from the river, the river Euphrates, even unto the uttermost sea shall your coast be."

In the fourth chapter of the book of Ruth it is revealed that when either a property or a responsibility was transferred from one person to another, it was officiated by the passing of the shoe (which, of course made it necessary to first remove it.) This practice is clearly seen in the following passage.

Ruth 4:7
"Now this was the manner in former time in Israel concerning redeeming and concerning changing, for to confirm all things; a man plucked off his shoe, and gave it to his neighbour: and this was a testimony in Israel."

So here is our first clue. In removing his shoes Moses was acknowledging that God is the rightful owner of the very ground that he stood on. More than that, I believe that Moses acknowledged God's ownership of everything he had.

God's Holiness cannot be compromised by the presence of rebellion or arrogance; His glory must be acknowledged. This is why confession (agreement with God) is so important when coming into the presence of the Lord. Confession shows respect for God and humility on the part of the worshiper.

Remember that **James 4:6** tells us that, *"… God resisteth the proud, but giveth grace unto the humble.."* And **Romans 13:2** says, *"Whosoever therefore resisteth the power, resisteth the* *ordinance of God: and they that resist shall receive to themselves damnation."*

Another principle to be discovered concerning the removal of the shoes is found in the fifth chapter of the book of Joshua.

Joshua 5:13-15

"And it came to pass, when Joshua was by Jericho, that he lifted up his eyes and looked, and, behold, there stood a man over against him with his sword drawn in his hand: and Joshua went unto him, and said unto him, Art thou for us, or for our adversaries?

And he said, Nay; but as captain of the host of the LORD am I now come. And Joshua fell on his face to the earth, and did worship, and said unto him, What saith my lord unto his servant?

And the captain of the LORD'S host said unto Joshua, Loose thy shoe from off thy foot; for the place whereon thou standest is holy. And Joshua did so."

Acts 10:34 teaches that God is no respecter of persons: That is, He doesn't play favorites. What the Lord was saying here is that He is sovereign and is not about our human agendas but rather exercises His own Will in the affairs of man. It just so happened that at this time the Israelites were acting in accordance with His Will and it is at those times that God is for us.

In taking off his shoes Moses was surrendering ownership of all he had, even his very life, to God as the rightful owner. Here we see humility and respect given to the ultimate authority, the King of all kings and the Lord of all lords. But sometimes the symbol points in another direction.

For example, consider when Moses led the Israelites out of Egypt. God gave him specific instructions regarding the eating of the Passover meal.

Exodus 12:11
"And thus shall ye eat it; with your loins girded, your shoes on your feet, and your staff in your hand; and ye shall eat it in haste: it is the LORD'S Passover."

Having the sandals on the feet, as with the girding of the loins, is idiomatic for being prepared for action. So, conversely, the removal of the sandals may speak of abiding, or in modern terms, "Take off your coat and stay awhile."

Being in the presence of God requires some changes in the life and demeanor of a person. Moses marveled that a bush could be burning but not be consumed. This speaks not of destruction, but of refinement.

Exodus 3:2
"… Behold, the bush burned with fire, and the bush was not consumed."

The Scriptures tell us that God is *a consuming fire*. But the fire of God is unto refinement. What is consumed in God's presence are those things that are contrary to His nature and when they are gone what remains is holy.

When the fires of regeneration work in the life of the believer he is transformed from glory to Glory. He finds his feet walking a new path as they fall into the prints of the One he now serves. The bush did not burn but blazed with the Glory of the presence of God.

Do you want to blaze with that Glory? Have you drawn near enough to God to be touched by the fire of His presence? Have you removed your sandals and do you abide in His Holy presence? Have you acknowledged Him as your Lord and confessed your need for Him? Have you submitted to Him and surrendered to Him your plans and your life? Take off you shoes and stay awhile.

Psalm 16:11

"Thou wilt shew me the path of life: in thy presence is fulness of joy; at thy right hand there are pleasures for evermore."

Chapter 5

THE BACK PARTS OF GOD

Exodus 33:18 – 34:1

"And he said, I beseech thee, shew me thy glory.

And he said, I will make all my goodness pass before thee, and I will proclaim the name of the LORD before thee; and will be gracious to whom I will be gracious, and will shew mercy on whom I will shew mercy.

And he said, Thou canst not see my face: for there shall no man see me, and live.

And the LORD said, Behold, there is a place by me, and thou shalt stand upon a rock:

And it shall come to pass, while my glory passeth by, that I will put thee in a cleft of the rock, and will cover thee with my hand while I pass by:

And I will take away mine hand, and thou shalt see my back parts: but my face shall not be seen..."

The Romans had a god called Janus. He had two faces. One faced forward and the other faced backward. The temple of Janus had open ends that were closed only during the Pax Romana or Peace of Rome. (That was the day that Augustus Caesar closed the doors of the temple of Janus located in the Forum – It's anniversary was on January 13th of each year.)

It is after the god Janus that January, the first month of our calendar year, is named. It seems that this is appropriate since the first month of the year stands at the nexus of the preceding and following years – that is, looking both forward and back.

In like manner, God's Word looks in both directions. Grace follows the Law and the Law precedes Grace. It was not yet time for the Face of God to be seen. First would have to come the Law in the form of the Levitical ordinances and the Ten Commandments.

It is generally accepted that Moses is a picture of the Law since it was given by God through him. For that very reason Moses could not behold the "face" or Grace of God. I believe that *the Law is the Back part of God*.

Only after the Law was given could the Face of God be seen. **Christ Jesus is the face of God** and He is the end (that is, the fulfillment) of the Law. It is the Face of God in Christ that puts to death the carnal self and regenerates the believer to life eternal. I believe that this is what God meant when He told Moses that, "*Thou canst not see my face: for there shall no man see me, and live.*"

It has been well said that "the Old Testament is the New Testament concealed and the New Testament is the Old Testament revealed." In the Old Testament salvation was believed to be in obeying the Law and performing ritual sacrifice. In the New Testament salvation is an act of Grace uniquely found in Christ Jesus. First comes the Law (Moses) then comes Grace (Jesus).

Moses (as the Law) is the back part of God. But it is the face that implies familiarity and relationship.

Jesus is the face of God.

Chapter 6

GLORIOUS DECEPTION

Genesis 25:20-34

"And Isaac was forty years old when he took Rebekah to wife, the daughter of Bethuel the Syrian of Padan-aram, the sister to Laban the Syrian.

And Isaac intreated the LORD for his wife, because she was barren: and the LORD was intreated of him, and Rebekah his wife conceived.

And the children struggled together within her; and she said, If it be so, why am I thus? And she went to inquire of the LORD.

And the LORD said unto her, Two nations are in thy womb, and two manner of people shall be separated from thy bowels; and the one people shall be stronger than the other people; and the elder shall serve the younger.

And when her days to be delivered were fulfilled, behold, there were twins in her womb.

And the first came out red, all over like an hairy garment; and they called his name Esau.

And after that came his brother out, and his hand took hold on Esau's heel; and his name was called Jacob: and Isaac was threescore years old when she bare them.

And the boys grew: and Esau was a cunning hunter, a man of the field; and Jacob was a plain man, dwelling in tents.

And Isaac loved Esau, because he did eat of his venison: but Rebekah loved Jacob.

And Jacob sod pottage: and Esau came from the field, and he was faint:

And Esau said to Jacob, Feed me, I pray thee, with that same red pottage; for I am faint: therefore was his name called Edom.

And Jacob said, Sell me this day thy birthright.

And Esau said, Behold, I am at the point to die: and what profit shall this birthright do to me?

And Jacob said, Swear to me this day; and he sware unto him: and he sold his birthright unto Jacob.

Then Jacob gave Esau bread and pottage of lentiles; and he did eat and drink, and rose up, and went his way: thus Esau despised his birthright."

On the surface these verses tell a tale of treachery and deceit. But as we look deeper into the record we find that it is a vehicle to communicate, once again, God's promise of restoration to a lost and dying race. Beneath the narrative, God has painted a wonderful picture of the conversion of the soul that leads to eternal glory for the believer.

First we notice that what appears to be deception is, in reality, prescribed by an all-knowing and sovereign God. In Genesis 25:23 we read that God told Rebecca that two nations struggled in her womb, and that the younger would rule the older. This prophecy looked beyond the conflict between the sons of Isaac and the sons of Ishmael and involves the personal struggle within all those who were to be converted by the indwelling of God's Holy Spirit.

Jacob, whose name means, "supplanter" or "restrainer", was younger than his brother Esau. But he was to receive all the authority and inheritance that was the natural birthright of the firstborn. That birthright does not belong to the flesh but to the re-born, whom Jacob represents in these verses. 1Cor 15:46 assures us that, *"first comes the natural, then the spiritual."*

Jacob represents the second born, or the new birth that entitles inheritance in the Kingdom of God. Esau, on the other hand, represents the first born or the natural man. This is why, in Genesis 25:27 Esau is called a man of the fields, belonging to the earth; while Jacob is called a "mild" man, a completed or mature man. (The word "mild" is a mistranslation of the Hebrew word "tam" which is better translated, "mature" or "complete".)

Esau's name is derived from the Hebrew word "Adam", which means red clay, the very thing that the natural man was made from. Note also that Esau is described as being hairy. The Hebrew word translated "hairy" also means "goat" and speaks of willfulness and rebellion; two things that the nature man is known for and are at odds with Divine viewpoint.

Now, we read in verse 29 that Esau came in from the hunt with a hearty appetite; an appetite so fierce that he proclaimed that he was faint. He begged Jacob for his red stew (the natural man craves the things of the earth). Jacob told Esau that he could have the stew in exchange for his birthright. Esau quickly agreed and told Jacob that he was about to die. This natural man was telling the truth because, as he said, in verse 32, "What profit shall this birthright do to me?"

In other words, the birthright is not for the natural, whom Esau represents, but for the reborn, represented by Jacob. Note that Esau had to agree to the exchange, even as the natural man has to agree to the coming of the Holy Spirit into the life. Note also that Jacob did not steal the birthright but purchased it just as Jesus paid for our reconciliation with His own red blood.

Thus the stage was set for the supplanter (the Holy Spirit) to usurp the position of the natural man as ruler in the life of the believer. The next step was to have Isaac bless the exchange or transfer of the birthright.

Chapter 27 of Genesis begins by telling us that Isaac's eyesight was failing due to his old age. It goes on to say how he asked his first born son, Esau, to kill some venison and make with it some savory stew. Isaac felt himself to be near death so he told Esau that he wanted to enjoy a savory meal and then to bless him as firstborn. All of this was overheard by Rebekah, Jacob's mother.

Now Rebekah had been told by God in Genesis 25:23 that the younger Jacob would rule over the elder Esau. So she called Jacob to her side and told him to pretend to be his brother Esau so that he would receive the blessing of the firstborn instead of his brother Esau. Jacob protested saying, "Esau is hairy while I am smooth skinned." He believed that his deception would be discovered and his father would curse him for it.

Rebekah applied goat skin to Jacob's hands and neck to deceive Isaac into accepting Jacob as Esau, his hairy firstborn.

Genesis 27:15-30
"And Rebekah took goodly raiment of her eldest son Esau, which were with her in the house, and put them upon Jacob her younger son:

And she put the skins of the kids of the goats upon his hands, and upon the smooth of his neck:

And she gave the savoury meat and the bread, which she had prepared, into the hand of her son Jacob.

And he came unto his father, and said, My father: and he said, Here am I; who art thou, my son?

And Jacob said unto his father, I am Esau thy firstborn; I have done according as thou badest me: arise, I pray thee, sit and eat of my venison, that thy soul may bless me.

And Isaac said unto his son, How is it that thou hast found it so quickly, my son? And he said, Because the LORD thy God brought it to me.

And Isaac said unto Jacob, Come near, I pray thee, that I may feel thee, my son, whether thou be my very son Esau or not.

And Jacob went near unto Isaac his father; and he felt him, and said, The voice is Jacob's voice, but the hands are the hands of Esau.

And he discerned him not, because his hands were hairy, as his brother Esau's hands: so he blessed him.

And he said, Art thou my very son Esau? And he said, I am.

And he said, Bring it near to me, and I will eat of my son's venison, that my soul may bless thee. And he brought it near to him, and he did eat: and he brought him wine, and he drank.

And his father Isaac said unto him, Come near now, and kiss me, my son.

And he came near, and kissed him: and he smelled the smell of his raiment, and blessed him, and said, See, the smell of my son is as the smell of a field which the LORD hath blessed:

Therefore God give thee of the dew of heaven, and the fatness of the earth, and plenty of corn and wine:

Let people serve thee, and nations bow down to thee: be lord over thy brethren, and let thy mother's sons bow down to thee: cursed be every one that curseth thee, and blessed be he that blesseth thee.

And it came to pass, as soon as Isaac had made an end of blessing Jacob, and Jacob was yet scarce gone out from the presence of Isaac his father, that Esau his brother came in from his hunting."

At this point in the record, Jacob became a symbol of Christ's "hypostatic union" (man and God in one person) as he represents the One who was to become our substitute.

2 Cor 5:21
"For he hath made him to be sin for us, who knew no sin; that we might be made the righteousness of God in him."

Remember that Rebekah covered Jacob's hands and neck with goat hair. This is highly significant since the goat is a symbol of sin and rebellion in the Scriptures. Can you see that Jacob presented himself to his father for the blessing as Esau (the carnal man) but he truly represented Jesus, the completed One.

Here God has given us a picture of the most glorious deception in all of human history. A picture of the perfect One who presented Himself to His Father in the guise of sinful humanity and thereby acquired, for all who would follow Him, the blessing of the Firstborn from the dead even as He is the firstborn of many brethren. (see **Romans 8:29**)

Chapter 7

WRESTLING WITH GOD AND MAN

Genesis 32:22-31

"And he rose up that night, and took his two wives, and his two women servants, and his eleven sons, and passed over the ford Jabbok.

And he took them, and sent them over the brook, and sent over that he had.

And Jacob was left alone; and there wrestled a man with him until the breaking of the day.

And when he saw that he prevailed not against him, he touched the hollow of his thigh; and the hollow of Jacob's thigh was out of joint, as he wrestled with him.

And he said, Let me go, for the day breaketh.

And he said, I will not let thee go, except thou bless me. And he said unto him, What is thy name? And he said, Jacob.

And he said, Thy name shall be called no more Jacob, but Israel: for as a prince hast thou power with God and with men, and hast prevailed.

And Jacob asked him, and said, Tell me, I pray thee, thy name. And he said, Wherefore is it that thou dost ask after my name? And he blessed him there.

And Jacob called the name of the place Peniel: for I have seen God face to face, and my life is preserved.

And as he passed over Penuel the sun rose upon him, and he halted upon his thigh."

What began in the 25th chapter of Genesis is completed in the 32nd chapter with the renaming of Jacob. Jacob left his home in Beersheba because he feared the anger of Esau. His brother had promised to kill him in return for "stealing" his birthright.

After 20 years of service to his crooked uncle Laban (Gen 31:38) in Padan aram, Jacob left with his families and all his holdings to go home and make his own way in the world.

While on the way back to Padan aram, Jacob decided to send word of his coming to his brother Esau but Jacob feared that Esau still desired to kill him. So he decided to bribe his brother by sending presents of livestock ahead in groups; hoping to soften his brother's hostility in stages.

One night he sent his wives and families across the brook called Jabbok and remained alone there. The record tells us that Jacob spent that night wrestling with a stranger who is thought to be the Angel of the Lord. The stranger could not better Jacob so he touched the hollow of Jacob's thigh to weaken him.

Then he demanded to be released. But Jacob would only release the him if the stranger would bless him. So the stranger asked Jacob his name. The answer was, "Jacob." This was tantamount to saying, "I am supplanter." Then the stranger said, from this time on you will be known as "Israel." Jacob received his blessing and released the man.

The first thing to notice in this account is the place of the struggle: At the brook called the Jabbok which empties into the Jordan River about mid-way between the Sea of Galilee and the Dead Sea. The name "Jabbok" means, "the emptying" because it literally empties into the Jordan River. But the real significance of the name is found in the fact that Jacob was emptied of himself in that place by the hand of God as the stranger.

It is also significant that the emptying took place near the Jordan River since the name Jordan means "descent" or "fall." The natural reason for the name Jordan is that its waters descend or fall from high up in northern Israel into the Dead Sea. However, it can also signify the fall from grace which brought on the Adamic curse.

Remember that the Jordan empties into the "Dead" Sea just as the fall from God's Grace resulted in death for Adam and all his children. Is this a stretch? Read on.

At the beginning of this encounter Jacob is simply himself, a man with a sin nature. Wrestling with God is something that we all do. For carnal man the struggle between Divine viewpoint and human viewpoint began in Eden and continues to this very day.

Jacob had many opportunities to respond to his uncle Laban's deceit in kind, but he maintained his integrity throughout his long service to him. Col 3:22:23 tells us to do everything as unto the Lord and this is what Jacob did. He wrestled with Laban against his own nature, which desires to pay harm for harm. And he wrestled with God who calls us to act with honor to even our enemy.

Thus he wrestled with man and with God and he prevailed. Therefore he had given evidence that he was ruled by God and not by his old or sin nature. Hence his name was changed from Jacob ("supplanter") to Israel ("ruled by God").

Now, about the hollow of Jacob's hip: The word translated "hip" is euphemistic for the "generative parts" or the genitals. To understand what is being pictured here we must look at the appropriate New Testament verse.

2 Cor 10:3-5
"... though we walk in the flesh, we do not war after the flesh:(For the weapons of our warfare are not carnal, but mighty through God to the pulling down of strong holds;) Casting down imaginations, and every high thing that exalteth itself against the knowledge of God, and bringing into captivity every thought to the obedience of Christ."

The Angel of the Lord struck the place of Jacob's ability to create those thoughts that are hostile to the will of God. Jacob had to be weakened in his carnal nature before he would be of any use to God. And so it is with all of Adam's rebellious children. This is a true blessing because until we are weakened in our human strength we will not accept God's strength.

Jacob's divine encounter ended with the breaking of the day. What a marvelous symbol of truth and understanding rising in a dark and lost soul. He exalted, "I have seen God face to face and my life is preserved." It is only when we look upon the face of God in Christ that we are delivered from sin and death to life eternal.

And the sun rose upon Jacob and he walked with a limp. What a glorious picture this is of Paul's statement in 2 Cor 2:10 that, *"when I am weak, then I am strong."* True strength is not found in self but in God.

At Jabbok, Jacob received not just the emptying of himself, but the infilling of God's Holy Spirit. This account is a living parable that prefigured the indwelling of the Holy Spirit that is promised to every follower of the Lord Jesus.

What Christian has not struggled with the details of life and the doubts and fears that are so much a part of man's lot? Who among us has been able to hear and respond to God's still small voice without His touch? He alone can deafen us to the discordant symphony of the world system that is so hostile to our gracious Creator God.

Be ever thankful, Christian, that the struggles and hardships you have endured have stripped you of the human arrogance and self-righteousness that we are all born with. He has brought you into His light and made you a partaker of the inheritance of the saints.

Praise His Holy Name.

Chapter 8

LIVING IN GOSHEN

The first time that I heard the word "Goshen" was in Disney comic books. One of Donald Duck's relatives often used the expression, "Land o' Goshen." I never knew that Goshen was a real place until I became a student of the Scriptures.

But as I grew in the knowledge of the Lord I started to look deeper and deeper into what God has intended to convey through the reading of His Word. It was then that I realized that not only was Goshen a real place but it was part of a real event. There is a deeper spiritual meaning in Goshen that has real significance for the believer today.

There is much to be learned from this living parable. When we look beneath the surface we will get a closer look at what God is telling us beyond the history of the event. Here is a true story of promise, of provision, of betrayal, and finally of salvation.

It began with Joseph as Egypt's most powerful ruler under Pharaoh inviting his family to leave drought stricken Canaan to live in the most fertile part of Egypt. It isn't very difficult to see in this invitation a picture of God the Father and God the Son inviting those who are lost out of the world and into the provision of His Kingdom.

Genesis 45:9-10

"Haste ye, and go up to my father, and say unto him, Thus saith thy son Joseph, God hath made me lord of all Egypt: come down unto me, tarry not: And thou shalt dwell in the land of Goshen, and thou shalt be near unto me, thou, and thy children, and thy children's children, and thy flocks, and thy herds, and all that thou hast ..."

It all began very nicely with Jacob and his sons experiencing the good life in the part of Egypt that had abundant water for themselves, their crops, and their livestock. So the family prospered and rapidly grew in number.

Genesis 47:27

"And Israel dwelt in the land of Egypt, in the country of Goshen; and they had possessions therein, and grew, and multiplied exceedingly."

Life was very good in Goshen, which was in the delta region of the Nile. But as their numbers grew another Pharaoh became increasingly fearful that they might present a threat to the stability and security of Egypt. And so, in total disregard for what had been promised the Hebrews by his predecessor, he decided to enslave them.

Exodus 1:8-13

"Now there arose up a new king over Egypt, which knew not Joseph.

And he said unto his people, Behold, the people of the children of Israel are more and mightier than we:

Come on, let us deal wisely with them; lest they multiply, and it come to pass, that, when there falleth out any war, they join also unto our enemies, and fight against us, and so get them up out of the land.

Therefore they did set over them taskmasters to afflict them with their burdens. And they built for Pharaoh treasure cities, Pithom and Raamses.

But the more they afflicted them, the more they multiplied and grew. And they were grieved because of the children of Israel.

And the Egyptians made the children of Israel to serve with rigour..."

For four centuries the sons of Jacob suffered under the heavy hand of Egypt. But in the fullness of time, God rose up a deliverer to draw His people out of captivity in Egypt. The name of that Deliverer was Moses (which means, "drawing out").

Under God's authority Moses went to Pharaoh and told him to let the people go. But seeing no reason to bow to the demands of Moses, Pharaoh refused. Then God sent the ten plagues to soften Pharaoh's resistance: Blood, frogs, lice, disease of beasts, boils, hail, locusts, darkness, and the death of the firstborn.

The Scriptures tell us that because of the Pharaoh's hardness of heart, there was suffering throughout Egypt but not in the land of Goshen.

Exodus 8:22-23

"And I will sever in that day the land of Goshen, in which my people dwell, that no swarms of flies shall be there; to the end thou mayest know that I am the LORD in the midst of the earth.

And I will put a division between my people and thy people: to morrow shall this sign be."

All who lived in the land of Goshen were safe. Why?

Could it be because the name "Goshen" means "Drawing Near"? (Confirmation of this meaning can be found on the web).[3] In Jesus God has offered an invitation to everyone to come to Him.

James 4:8
"Draw nigh to God, and he will draw nigh to you…"

All people are seeking the same two things. Who can deny that we all want happiness and security? The only difference is in the way and the means by which these things are obtained. Regardless of culture, ethnicity, or world view, everything that human beings strive for is to that end.

Some seek happiness and security through wealth. Some think that position and fame will secure it for them. Others search for identity and meaning in life. And still others busy themselves in perverse endeavors that are self-defeating.

The Scriptures tell us that apart from God the pursuit of happiness is an exercise in futility. Sooner or later we all find out that the best we can hope for is that life's pleasures might outweigh life's pains. All earthly delights carry with them a price that is often higher than their true value.

John 16:33
"These things I have spoken unto you, that in me ye might have peace. In the world ye shall have tribulation: but be of good cheer; I have overcome the world."

---

3 www.blueletterbible.org/tmp_dir/words

Thankfully God has offered to partner with us that we might experience, in Him, happiness and security that do not rely on our abilities or our circumstances. Far better is the happiness and security that He has already paid for and graciously offers to all for free.

Psalm 16:11
"… In [God's] presence is fullness of joy; At [His] right hand are pleasures forevermore."

God has made it possible for us live in Goshen just as the Hebrews did.

Hebrews 10:22
"… let us draw near with a true heart in full assurance of faith, having our hearts sprinkled from an evil conscience and our bodies washed with pure water."

Jesus is the Way, the Truth, and the Life.

Hebrews 7:19
"… for the law made nothing perfect; on the other hand, there is the bringing in of a better hope, through which we draw near to God."

Through prayer and spending time in God's Word, and by praising Him in song and speech we draw near to God and He draws near to us.

In Christ, He promised to be present whenever two or three are gathered together in His Name. We call this, "God talk".

Psalm 145:18 tells us that, *"The LORD is near to all who call upon Him, To all who call upon Him in truth."*

When we call out to Him we are delivered from all those things that the plagues of Egypt represent: Torments, depression, insecurity, hopelessness, loneliness etc.

Phil 4:6-7
"Be careful for nothing; but in every thing by prayer and supplication with thanksgiving let your requests be made known unto God. And the peace of God, which passeth all understanding, shall keep your hearts and minds through Christ Jesus."

So when you are discouraged and don't know what to do, just praise the Lord and speak His Word, and He will see you through the difficult times. He promised to never leave you nor forsake you; and He has proven Himself to be faithful down through the centuries.

Chapter 9

CROSSING OVER

John 5:24
"Verily, verily, I say unto you, He that heareth my word, and believeth on him that sent me, hath everlasting life, and shall not come into condemnation; but is passed from death unto life."

There is a program on TV hosted by John Edwards called "Crossing Over." It is a show where he claims to relay messages from the dead to the living. I think it is an appropriate title because from the earliest of times man has likened the journey from this life into the next with the crossing of a river.

It seems that all major cultures have a mythology concerning the transition from this world into the next by crossing a river. The Egyptians, for example, had the river Nile. But perhaps the best known are the river Styx of Greek and Roman origin and the river Jordan of Hebrew origin.

These are metaphorical rivers of death. Just as death is the boundary or dividing point between this world and the next, these rivers separate the world of the living from the world of the dead. In the case of the river Styx it was considered to be the boundary between the earth and Hell. So where did this idea come from?

The river Styx was a real river that flowed through Arcadia, which is in Greece, and disappeared into the ground on its way to the sea. Its disappearance into the ground made it appropriate as the river that formed the boundary between this world and Hades, which was thought to be the place of the "shades."

It was believed that when we leave this life we become shades and live in an underworld in a weakened state, such as in a dream. The soul of the dead was thought to cross the river Styx to enter Hades. And the only way across was by the ferryman Charon who demanded payment in silver for his service.

Hence the corpse was to be buried with a silver coin (called an "obol") under the tongue or between the teeth. I find it interesting that the crossing required payment on the part of the deceased and that it had to be in silver. (Silver is the Bible's symbol for redemption).

When the soul crossed the Styx into Hades, it would abandon all hope because the way back was barred by the dragon-tailed dog Cerberus. Afterlife for the ancients was nothing to look forward to. It's no wonder that their anthem was, "eat, drink, and be merry; for tomorrow we die."

The concept of a river dividing the living from the dead or life from the afterlife may well have begun with the Hebrews. The word "Hebrew", itself, means "to cross over."

As previously stated Strong's lexicon shows that the word "Jordan" literally means, "to fall or descend". And we know from the Torah that the river Jordan was literally the dividing point between the wilderness and the promised land of milk and honey.

While the pagan and the unbeliever still have to cross the metaphorical river of death on Charon's ferry, those who follow Jesus can safely cross over at His expense and enter into paradise. The Lord has painted for us a great and glorious picture of the believer's crossing in the book of Joshua. Let's look at it and see it afresh.

Before I exegete these passages, understand that the name Joshua is a Hebrew word that means "God saves," or "sets free." The name "Jesus" is the Hellenized version of that same name. Therefore Joshua is a "type" of Jesus.

Joshua 3:1-13

And Joshua rose early in the morning; and they removed from Shittim, and came to Jordan, he and all the children of Israel, and lodged there before they passed over.

And it came to pass after three days, that the officers went through the host;

And they commanded the people, saying, When ye see the ark of the covenant of the LORD your God, and the priests the Levites bearing it, then ye shall remove from your place, and go after it.

Yet there shall be a space between you and it, about two thousand cubits by measure: come not near unto it, that ye may know the way by which ye must go: for ye have not passed this way heretofore.

And Joshua said unto the people, Sanctify yourselves: for to morrow the LORD will do wonders among you.

And Joshua spake unto the priests, saying, Take up the ark of the covenant, and pass over before the people. And they took up the ark of the covenant, and went before the people.

And the LORD said unto Joshua, This day will I begin to magnify thee in the sight of all Israel, that they may know that, as I was with Moses, so I will be with thee.

And thou shalt command the priests that bear the ark of the covenant, saying, When ye are come to the brink of the water of Jordan, ye shall stand still in Jordan.

And Joshua said unto the children of Israel, Come hither, and hear the words of the LORD your God.

And Joshua said, Hereby ye shall know that the living God is among you, and that he will without fail drive out from before you the Canaanites, and the Hittites, and the Hivites, and the Perizzites, and the Girgashites, and the Amorites, and the Jebusites.

Behold, the ark of the covenant of the Lord of all the earth passeth over before you into Jordan.

Now therefore take you twelve men out of the tribes of Israel, out of every tribe a man.

And it shall come to pass, as soon as the soles of the feet of the priests that bear the ark of the LORD, the Lord of all the earth, shall rest in the waters of Jordan, that the waters of Jordan shall be cut off from the waters that come down from above; and they shall stand upon an heap.

Now here are the verses that reveal God's promise of salvation in living parable:

Joshua 3:14-17

And it came to pass, when the people removed from their tents, to pass over Jordan, and the priests bearing the ark of the covenant before the people;

And as they that bare the ark were come unto Jordan, and the feet of the priests that bare the ark were dipped in the brim of the water, (for Jordan overfloweth all his banks all the time of harvest,)

That the waters which came down from above stood and rose up upon an heap very far from the city (uwr: to open the eyes) Adam, that is beside (opposite to) Zaretan (tserador: to pierce or puncture): and those that came down toward the sea of the plain, even the salt sea, failed, and were cut off (the Adamic cursed has been breached by the Cross of Christ) and the people passed over right against Jericho. (fragrance)

And the priests that bare the ark of the covenant of the LORD stood firm on dry ground in the midst of Jordan, and all the Israelites passed over on dry ground, until all the people were passed clean over Jordan.

It was Yeshua (Joshua) who led the children of Israel across the Jordan into the Promised land flowing with milk and honey (a symbol of prosperity).

The Jordan is an appropriate symbol for the barrier between the Earth and Heaven because it is precisely the Fall from God's grace that separates us from the presence of God in eternity. Remember, the fall or decent of the waters of the Jordan empty into the Dead Sea. It can be seen here that it is man's separation from God that brought about death.

This brings me to a point of great importance that I believe needs to be proclaimed from the pulpit today. There is a prevailing thought by many (even among believers) that good works can pay the price required to enter Heaven. This misunderstanding persists even though many preach against the value of good works in saving a lost soul. The idea of a set of scales where a person's bad deeds are weighed against their good deeds as determining their eternal destiny still exists in the minds of many.

It is true that good deeds will validate the saved condition of the born-again. But it is not human good that will get you across the Jordan and into the Promised land. Good deeds have no power to get anybody into Heaven and, here is a shocker for many: bad deeds have no power to keep anybody out of Heaven. It is solely the rejection of Christ's offer of salvation that bars one from Heaven: That it truly the unpardonable sin.

In short, entry into Heaven, according to the Bible, has nothing to do with the energy of the flesh or human morality. The Scriptures tell us that without the shedding of blood there can be no remission of sin. They also tell us that the blood of bulls and goats are not capable of saving us. Only the blood of the Lamb of God is able to propitiate, to make adequate payment and restore a lost soul to God.

Hebrews 10:4
For it is not possible that the blood of bulls and of goats should take away sins.

The Lord Jesus is the High Priest who first put His foot into the waters of the river of death that it might open up a way for the people of God to cross over into the Promised land.

Before the saving works of Jesus, the dead had to pay their own way; and that way led only to Hell. But praise God, all who believe can be assured of crossing over into Heaven. The way has been made through the river of death for us by the Lord Jesus Christ. He has paid our way for us with the silver coin of His own Blood.

Because God so loved the world that He gave His only begotten Son, the believer's guide into eternity is not an ill tempered ferryman demanding a silver coin for his service, but rather a great High Priest who lovingly paid your passage and mine with His own precious Life. This and only this is the key to salvation and the promises of God.

When I look beneath the surface of God's Word, I marvel at the Glory of the Lord and have to agree with the Apostle Paul when he said:

Romans 11:33-36
"O the depth of the riches both of the wisdom and knowledge of God! how unsearchable are his judgments, and his ways past finding out! For who hath known the mind of the Lord? or who hath been his counsellor? Or who hath first given to him, and it shall be recompensed unto him again? For of him, and through him, and to him, are all things: to whom be glory for ever. "

Chapter 10

THE PROMISE

Isaiah 9:6-7

"... and his name shall be called Wonderful, Counsellor, The mighty God, The everlasting Father, The Prince of Peace. Of the increase of his government and peace there shall be no end, upon the throne of David, and upon his kingdom, to order it, and to establish it with judgment and with justice from henceforth even for ever. The zeal of the LORD of hosts will perform this."

Six thousand years ago, according to the Biblical record, Eve, the first woman, followed a recommendation made by a deceiving snake and willingly violated a Divine command. Although she was the one who listened to the snake, it was her husband, Adam, who was responsible for the transgression. Incidentally, it remains to this day the responsibility of the husband to guide his family according to the mandates of God.

When Adam followed his wife into rebellion, he shattered the protection that God had placed around them and they found themselves in a new and different world; a world that was harsh and hostile to them. But that wasn't the end of the story.

Just before they left Eden God, in His mercy, made them a promise. He promised in Genesis 3:15 that the serpent would not rule forever; that from woman (in the flesh) there would come a deliverer who would defeat the serpent and restore man to Divine favor.

Gen 3:15

And I will put enmity between thee and the woman, and between thy seed and her seed; it shall bruise thy head, and thou shalt bruise his heel.

This is perhaps the most profound promise in the entire Bible. It is the very heart of the Gospel message: That fallen, lost man would one day be redeemed by a Savior and returned to his former blessed state.

And because man's memory is short, God placed reminders of His promise throughout the Bible to encourage us and give us hope. God wants us know that He is still in charge and that He has not abandoned us to the Devil. Here in the Biblical account of David and Goliath is perhaps the best known of all those reminders.

The record begins with the Biblical struggle between Israelites and their old enemies the Philistines.

1 Sam 17:1-6

"Now the Philistines gathered together their armies to battle, and were gathered together at Shochoh, which belongeth to Judah, and pitched between Shochoh and Azekah, in Ephesdammim.

And Saul and the men of Israel were gathered together, and pitched by the valley of Elah, and set the battle in array against the Philistines.

And the Philistines stood on a mountain on the one side, and Israel stood on a mountain on the other side: and there was a valley between them.

And there went out a champion out of the camp of the Philistines, named Goliath, of Gath, whose height was six cubits and a span.

And he had an helmet of brass upon his head, and he was armed with a coat of mail; and the weight of the coat was five thousand shekels of brass.

And he had greaves of brass upon his legs, and a target of brass between his shoulders."

There are, recorded in this chapter, various symbols to be noted in what is known as the meta-narrative (the story within the story):

1. The battlefield is the world.

2. The armies are representative of the forces of light and the forces of darkness.

3. In the space separating the two armies there stands the fearsome giant Goliath cursing and taunting Israel (those ruled by God). The name Goliath comes from a root that means "to uncover", and he is from Gath which means "to tread or press." It is the function and nature of the Devil to remove the covering of God from the sons of Adam.

4. Behind the giant, confident of victory, stand the Philistines, a Hebrew word that means, "those who roll in the dust."

Is there no one worthy to stand against the enemy on behalf of the army of the Lord? Yes, the young shepherd David. The record continues as David enters the scene.

1 Sam 17:17-22

"And Jesse said unto David his son, Take now for thy brethren an ephah of this parched corn, and these ten loaves, and run to the camp to thy brethren;

And carry these ten cheeses unto the captain of their thousand, and look how thy brethren fare, and take their pledge.

Now Saul, and they, and all the men of Israel, were in the valley of Elah, fighting with the Philistines.

And David rose up early in the morning, and left the sheep with a keeper, and took, and went, as Jesse had commanded him; and he came to the trench, as the host was going forth to the fight, and shouted for the battle.

For Israel and the Philistines had put the battle in array, army against army.

And David left his carriage in the hand of the keeper of the carriage, and ran into the army, and came and saluted his brethren."

While the two armies faced each other, Jesse sent his youngest son David to the battlefield to take bread to his brothers to sustain them. But when David arrived, he found the army of Israel paralyzed by a challenge they could not meet.

When David found that not one of the warriors in King Saul's army was up to the challenge, he inquired of the men about the problem.

1 Sam 17:23-25

"And as he talked with them, behold, there came up the champion, the Philistine of Gath, Goliath by name, out of the armies of the Philistines, and spake according to the same words: and David heard them.

And all the men of Israel, when they saw the man, fled from him, and were sore afraid.

And the men of Israel said, Have ye seen this man that is come up? surely to defy Israel is he come up: and it shall be, that the man who killeth him, the king will enrich him with great riches, and will give him his daughter, and make his father's house free in Israel."

David asked, "Who is this uncircumcised Philistine that he should defy the army of the living God?" And in verse 26 He asked, "What shall be given to the one who defeats the giant Goliath?" The promise of the hand of King Saul's daughter seemed to interest David and he promised to defeat the giant on behalf of Israel.

1 Sam 17:32-39

"And David said to Saul, Let no man's heart fail because of him; thy servant will go and fight with this Philistine.

And Saul said to David, Thou art not able to go against this Philistine to fight with him: for thou art but a youth, and he a man of war from his youth.

And David said unto Saul, Thy servant kept his father's sheep, and there came a lion, and a bear, and took a lamb out of the flock:

And I went out after him, and smote him, and delivered it out of his mouth: and when he arose against me, I caught him by his beard, and smote him, and slew him.

Thy servant slew both the lion and the bear: and this uncircumcised Philistine shall be as one of them, seeing he hath defied the armies of the living God.

David said moreover, The LORD that delivered me out of the paw of the lion, and out of the paw of the bear, he will deliver me out of the hand of this Philistine. And Saul said unto David, Go, and the LORD be with thee.

And Saul armed David with his armour, and he put an helmet of brass upon his head; also he armed him with a coat of mail.

And David girded his sword upon his armour, and he assayed to go; for he had not proved it. And David said unto Saul, I cannot go with these; for I have not proved them. And David put them off him."

David accepted Goliath's challenge on behalf of his kinsmen but refused to use the King's armor or his weapons. (*For the weapons of our warfare are not carnal, but mighty through God to the pulling down of strong holds ...*) **2 Cor 10:4**

David chose to use only a sling and smooth stones against the might of the Philistines' champion.

1 Sam 17:40-51
"And he took his staff in his hand, and chose him five smooth stones out of the brook, and put them in a shepherd's bag which he had, even in a scrip; and his sling was in his hand: and he drew near to the Philistine.

And the Philistine came on and drew near unto David; and the man that bare the shield went before him.

And when the Philistine looked about, and saw David, he disdained him: for he was but a youth, and ruddy, and of a fair countenance.

And the Philistine said unto David, Am I a dog, that thou comest to me with staves? And the Philistine cursed David by his gods.

And the Philistine said to David, Come to me, and I will give thy flesh unto the fowls of the air, and to the beasts of the field.

Then said David to the Philistine, Thou comest to me with a sword, and with a spear, and with a shield: but I come to thee in the name of the LORD of hosts, the God of the armies of Israel, whom thou hast defied.

This day will the LORD deliver thee into mine hand; and I will smite thee, and take thine head from thee; and I will give the carcases of the host of the Philistines this day unto the fowls of the air, and to the wild beasts of the earth; that all the earth may know that there is a God in Israel.

And all this assembly shall know that the LORD saveth not with sword and spear: for the battle is the LORD's, and he will give you into our hands.

And it came to pass, when the Philistine arose, and came and drew nigh to meet David, that David hasted, and ran toward the army to meet the Philistine.

And David put his hand in his bag, and took thence a stone, and slang it, and smote the Philistine in his forehead, that the stone sunk into his forehead; and he fell upon his face to the earth.

So David prevailed over the Philistine with a sling and with a stone, and smote the Philistine, and slew him; but there was no sword in the hand of David.

Therefore David ran, and stood upon the Philistine, and took his sword, and drew it out of the sheath thereof, and slew him, and cut off his head therewith. And when the Philistines saw their champion was dead, they fled."

With a simple sling David placed one smooth stone into the brain of the giant and Goliath fell, then David removed his head. With the defeat of Goliath, the Philistines were discouraged and took flight.

Now we are ready to look beneath the surface of the narrative and discover the promise so skillfully placed within this historical record by our great God.

In verses 17 to 22, a father sends his son into a great battle to take bread to his brothers. Consider this:

1. Strong's lexicon defines the name Jesse, David's father, as "I Exist". (Strong's compares the Hebrew word "hayah" to God's declaration to Moses from the burning bush, "I Am that I Am".)

2. Strong's lexicon defines the name David, the name of Jesse's son, as "Beloved."

The promise was once more affirmed: - Jesse (I AM, from *yesh:* I exist) sent his son David (beloved) to the place of battle (the world) to take bread to his brothers. This is the Gospel of Jesus in a nutshell. ***Simply stated, God sent His Son into the Earth to bring the Bread of Life to His brothers.*** But there is more.

In verses 40 to 51, David defeated Goliath and won the battle for God's people. The enemy was decapitated, which can mean that the Devil has lost his headship and the people of God have been restored to fellowship with the Father.

And finally, in verse 25, we can see David's reward for his victory:

1 Sam 17:25
"Now the Israelites had been saying, "Do you see how this man keeps coming out? He comes out to defy Israel. The king will give great wealth to the man who kills him. He will also give him his daughter in marriage and will exempt his father's family from taxes in Israel."

David won the riches of the Kingdom, a Bride, and exemption from taxes for his whole family. So in this brief account God has hidden His promise for all who would mine His Word as for silver and gold. Can you see it?

I AM that I AM sent His Beloved Son into the world to take the bread of life to those who believe. The Beloved defeated the Enemy and removed his head. The Devil no longer rules those who are heirs to the Kingdom.

And the Beloved won the daughter of the King as a Bride. The Bride has access to the riches of the Kingdom and exemption from Divine judgment. What a glorious chapter this is in the Word of God. God has left His promise to us in many living parables throughout His Word – this is just one of them.

What a mighty God we serve; all honor and praise and glory be to You Lord Jesus for You have overcome the enemy by the power of Your love for Your people – You have called us and we are Yours.

Chapter 11

JEHOSHAPHAT'S BATTLE

Isaiah 41:10 *Fear not, for I am with you; Be not dismayed, for I am your God. I will strengthen you, Yes, I will help you, I will uphold you with My righteous right hand.'*

About three and a half thousand years ago, Moses stood on the shore of the Red Sea and called on God to deliver a terrified Israel from what seemed to be certain death. Behind them, Pharaoh's army; before them a great expanse of water deep enough to drown a man and his horse.

As Moses looked over his shoulder towards the Egyptians, he must have seen the pillar of cloud that God had placed between them and the fleeing Israelites.

Exodus 14:19-20
"…the Angel of God, who went before the camp of Israel, moved and went behind them; and the pillar of cloud went from before them and stood behind them. So it came between the camp of the Egyptians and the camp of Israel. Thus it was a cloud and darkness to the one, and it gave light by night to the other, so that the one did not come near the other all that night."

Moses had told the people, "Stand still and behold the salvation of the Lord." And then the children of Israel witnessed the first miracle of their exodus as the sea was parted and they crossed it on dry land.

Exodus 14:21-23
"... Moses stretched out his hand over the sea; and the LORD caused the sea to go back by a strong east wind all that night, and made the sea into dry land, and the waters were divided. So the children of Israel went into the midst of the sea on the dry ground, and the waters were a wall to them on their right hand and on their left. And the Egyptians pursued and went after them into the midst of the sea, all Pharaoh's horses, his chariots, and his horsemen.

About 600 years later a king of Judah, in the Davidic line, faced another fearful situation. It seemed to him that he and the men of Israel faced certain death at the hands of a fearful enemy who greatly outnumbered them. His name was Jehoshaphat (Hebrew for *"Jehovah will judge or vindicate or defend"*), and he was King David's great, great, great grandson.

Jehoshaphat and his father, Asa, had rid the kingdom of paganism thus reestablishing the separation between them and the nations. Perhaps this was the main reason that the Moabites and their allies, the Ammonites, and the men of Mt. Seir decided to drive them out of the land as recorded in Chapter 20 of 2Chronicles.

2 Chron 20:1-2
"It came to pass after this also, that the children of Moab, and the children of Ammon, and with them other beside the Ammonites, came against Jehoshaphat to battle. Then there came some that told Jehoshaphat, saying, There cometh a great multitude against

*thee from beyond the sea on this side **Syria**; and, behold, they be **Hazazon-tamar**, which is **En-gedi**.*

In keeping with the meanings of the names in the original language:

Syria refers to "an elevated place" as in "prideful."

Hazazon (Hebrew "chatsats") refers to "piercing or wounding."

Tamar means "to be erect."

En Gedi refers to a young kid or goat and may be a symbol of "willfulness."

As these names are viewed from their Hebrew perspective, rather than as simple labels, it becomes easy to infer that these enemies issued forth from a nature that is arrogant, intent on wounding the upright, and is willful and rebellious. These same characteristics can be found in the enemies of Christ to this day.

Fearful of the strength of the approaching army, Jehoshaphat called the inhabitants of Judah to the House of God to petition the God of their fathers for deliverance from this threat.

2 Chron 20:3-9

*"And Jehoshaphat feared, and set himself to seek the LORD, and proclaimed **a fast** throughout all Judah.*

And Judah gathered themselves together, to ask help of the LORD; even out of all the cities of Judah they came to seek the LORD.

And Jehoshaphat stood in the congregation of Judah and Jerusalem, in the house of the LORD, before the new court,

And said, O LORD God of our fathers, art not thou God in heaven? And rulest not thou over all the kingdoms of the heathen? And in thine hand is there not power and might, so that none is able to withstand thee?

Art not thou our God, who didst drive out the inhabitants of this land before thy people Israel, and gavest it to the seed of Abraham thy friend for ever?

And they dwelt therein, and have built thee a sanctuary therein for thy name, saying,

*If, when evil cometh upon us, as the sword, judgment, or pestilence, or famine, we stand before this **house**, and in thy presence, (for thy name is in this house,) and cry unto thee in our affliction, then thou wilt hear and help."*

The fast in this passage did not necessarily refer to abstaining from food. Such abstinence no doubt occurred. However, the true sense of the word here is: To drop whatever it is you're doing and put aside your own plans and projects in order to come together in a concentrated effort for the good of the nation, the congregation, or the family, as an act of holiness. The word "house" in this passage is from the Hebrew word "bayith," which refers to a "family" in the broadest sense.

The people of Judah cried out to God to save them from the great company that marched against them. They confessed that they were terrified and did not know what to do but they looked to the God of their fathers for deliverance. As all Judah came together at the Temple a prophet named Jahaziel addressed the congregation in the Spirit of the Lord.

2 Chron 20:12-15

"O our God, wilt thou not judge them? for we have no might against this great company that cometh against us; **neither know we what to do: but our eyes are upon thee***.*

And all Judah stood before the LORD, with their little ones, their wives, and their children.

Then upon Jahaziel the son of Zechariah, the son of Benaiah, the son of Jeiel, the son of Mattaniah, a Levite of the sons of Asaph, came the Spirit of the LORD in the midst of the congregation;

And he said, 'Hearken ye, all Judah, and ye inhabitants of Jerusalem, and thou king Jehoshaphat, thus saith the LORD unto you, be not afraid nor dismayed by reason of this great multitude; for the battle is not yours, but God's.'"

The Jahaziel in this passage comes at the end of a Levitical family line. As we trace the meanings of the names from Mattaniah, the first in the lineage, we have:

1. **Mattaniah**: "A gift from God." Speaks of **Salvation**.
2. **Jeiel**: "God sweeps or carries away." Speaks of **Sanctification**.
3. **Benaiah**: "The Lord builds or repairs." Speaks of **Regeneration**.
4. **Zechariah**: "To remember or be mindful of the Lord." Speaks of **Dedication**.
5. **Jahaziel**: "Vision or perception of the Almighty." Speaks of **Relationship/Intimacy**.

Considering the Hebrew meaning of the names of Jahaziel's ancestors it is not difficult to see a picture of God's hand in bringing the believer to spiritual maturity.

First comes the Cross, then old things pass and the believer is set apart unto the Lord. Next all things are made new or regenerated and then the believer is dedicated to the Lord and seeks His will. These steps lead the believer to knowledge of the Holy and intimacy with God.

As a Levite, Jahaziel is of the priestly line and uniquely qualified to speak the oracles of God. He encourages the people as he tells them that the battle is the Lord's.

2 Chron 20:16-17

"To morrow go ye down against them: behold, they come up by the cliff of Ziz; and ye shall find them at the end of the brook, before the wilderness of Jeruel. Ye shall not need to fight in this battle: set yourselves, stand ye still, and see the salvation of the LORD with you, O Judah and Jerusalem: Fear not, nor be dismayed; to morrow go out against them: for the LORD will be with you."

Jehoshaphat and all the people rejoiced and praised God for His promise of victory. Then the following morning the army of the Lord rose up and marched confidently toward their encounter with a formidable enemy.

2 Chron 20:20-21

"And they rose early in the morning, and went forth into the wilderness of Tekoa: and as they went forth, Jehoshaphat stood and said, Hear me, O Judah, and ye inhabitants of Jerusalem; Believe in the LORD your God, so shall ye be established; believe his prophets, so shall ye prosper. And when he had consulted with the people, he appointed singers unto the LORD, and that should praise the beauty of holiness, as they went out before the army, and to say, Praise the LORD; for his mercy endureth for ever."

Jehoshaphat appointed singers to go ahead of the Israelite army to praise the Lord for His mercy, and as they marched toward the battle their enemies began to fight and kill each other. So the victory was won without a single Israelite casualty.

2 Chron 20:22-24

"And when they began to sing and to praise, the LORD set ambushments against the children of Ammon, Moab, and mount Seir, which were come against Judah; and they were smitten. For the children of Ammon and Moab stood up against the inhabitants of mount Seir, utterly to slay and destroy them: and when they had made an end of the inhabitants of Seir, every one helped to destroy another. And when Judah came toward the watch tower in the wilderness, they looked unto the multitude, and, behold, they were dead bodies fallen to the earth, and none escaped."

Instead of meeting the fierce opposition of an enemy determined to destroy them, the Israelites were surprised to see that their enemy had turned on himself. Instead of engaging in a mighty battle with an enemy that greatly outnumbered them, Jehoshaphat's men spent the next three days collecting the spoils of their victory.

2 Chron 20:25

"And when Jehoshaphat and his people came to take away the spoil of them, they found among them in abundance both riches with the dead bodies, and precious jewels, which they stripped off for themselves, more than they could carry away: and they were three days in gathering of the spoil, it was so much."

When viewed beyond the traditional interpretation and seen as God has presented it, this incident conveys a great message of comfort and encouragement for the believer. As already said, Israel is a compound Hebrew word that literally means, "Ruled by the Mighty One." They are of the people of God and they represent the followers of Christ today.

Beyond the history of the Biblical account in Jehoshaphat's battle there is much of spiritual significance that God has given us in metaphor. First it is to be remembered that Adam has left us a fallen world and that much of what we battle with in the world is a consequence of that Fall.

Eph 6:12
"For we wrestle not against flesh and blood, but against principalities, against powers, against the rulers of the darkness of this world, against spiritual wickedness in high places."

So often the battles recorded in the Scriptures are representative of the spiritual struggles that we all go through. The Lord has recorded these things with His words so that we might have a defence against what we cannot overcome in our own strength.

2 Cor 10:4
"For the weapons of our warfare are not carnal, but mighty through God to the pulling down of strong holds."

In naming the nations that move on Israel, the Lord has told us something about spiritual forces that torment us. Ammon means "to overshadow" and speaks of intimidation. Moab means "illegitimate" and speaks of falseness. Mount Seir comes from a root that means "devil" and speaks of rebellion.

The details recorded in this historical event teach us that when we are surrounded by troubles or dangers so that we don't know what to do, we should turn to the Lord and keep our eyes on Him; He is far better equipped for the battle than we.

When Jehoshaphat appointed the singers to go ahead of the army it was the Levites that he chose. This is significant because the Hebrew word "levite" derives from a root that means "attached" or "united." These were the people who stood up to praise God in a time of great trouble or danger. People who humbled themselves to expose their minds to the Lord; people who agreed with the Lord and leaned on Him to meet their needs.

The praises of the Levites toward God, as they march into the battle, represent the trust and thanksgiving given to God in the midst of the trials and tribulations that so often befall us. As we praise Him and thank Him for His provision, our problems don't seem so large any more.

As he approached the battle, Jehoshaphat found that the enemy had already been defeated and there was nothing left but to enjoy the fruits of victory. In this delivery from trouble, God has shown us something about the way troubles can work against themselves when we hand the battle over to the Lord.

In Genesis we are told that the serpent will eat the dust of the earth. Satan is a scavenger and it is his function to feed on carrion. When God's people show themselves to be partakers of the life of the living God by trusting in Him and praising Him, they became distasteful to the enemy. As the lord of decay, Satan only has a taste for things that are dead; which is our spiritual condition before accepting God's gift of salvation which is found only in Christ Jesus.

When God is praised, He is able to deliver us and our troubles seem to dissolve.

Romans 8:28

"And we know that all things work together for good to them that love God, to them who are the called according to his purpose."

Our troubles, which are ultimately a consequence of the Fall, are in alignment with Satan and as such are dead things. So just as Jehoshaphat's enemies slew each other, when a believer is praising God, troubles seem to go away.

Here in summary is a song showing that victory over our troubles is found only in the Lord. (Notice the recurring theme, "Oh God, we keep our eyes on You!":)

Jehoshaphat Was Praying
When The News Came To His Ears
The Enemy Was On The Move,
And He Was Struck With Fear
He Cried, "Oh God, What Will We Do?"

The Enemy Is Strong And Fierce,
Destructive Beyond Measure
He Comes Up From Beyond The Sea,
And Torment Is His Pleasure
But God Is With His People
And He Will Not Let Them Fall
His Mighty Hand Will Cover Them
And Keep Them From All Harm
Oh God, We Keep Our Eyes On You
God Of Our Salvation, Faithful And True

This Son Of David Called A Fast
To Seek The Lord's Direction
The People Put Aside Their Works,

And Gathered At The Temple
They Prayed, "Oh God, What Will We Do?"

Then The Spirit Of The Lord Spoke Through
The Son Of Zechariah
Take Heed To What I Say
And Do Not Fear This Trial Of Fire
I Will Deliver You,
From Your Afflictions
Of God, We Keep Our Eyes On You

The Morning Sun Arose Upon
A People Strong And Free
Their Shields Reflected In The Dew
That Hung On Every Tree
They Sang The Praises
Of Their Redeemer
Oh God, We Keep Our Eyes On You

The Levites Went Before Them
Singing Glory To The Lord
They Met The Foe,
But He Was Struck,
And From Within Destroyed
The Lord Preserved Them,
As They Praised His Name
Oh God, We Keep Our Eyes On You

So when you are in trouble
And you don't know what to do,
Just praise the Lord
And speak His word
And He will fight for you,

You will behold
The mighty hand of God,
You will behold
The salvation of the Lord.[4]

No matter how impossible the circumstances appear to be, always remember that our hope is in the Lord.

John 14:1
"Let not your heart be troubled; you believe in God, believe also in Me."

Phil 4:6
"Be careful for nothing; but in every thing by prayer and supplication with thanksgiving let your requests be made known unto God. And the peace of God, which passeth all understanding, shall keep your hearts and minds through Christ Jesus."

---

4 "Victory Is In The Lord." Savior's Robe c 2004

Chapter 12

EBENEZER

Isaiah 28:16
"… Behold, I lay in Zion for a foundation a stone, a tried stone, a precious corner stone, a sure foundation: he that believeth shall not make haste."

A stone is laid in Zion. What Stone? Scripture teaches us that Christ is that Stone but have you ever wondered why? Where did this idea to refer to Jesus as a stone come from?

A stone has some very distinct characteristics that make it a completely appropriate symbol for Christ. A stone is solid and durable; it suggests stability and permanence. It is used in construction and tools for shaping and it is part of a larger object – a rock or cliff.

A stone is also appropriate because it has many different shapes. When you think of a stone you don't think of a particular shape. Rather you think of its characteristics or qualities. So it is with Jesus; it is not His shape or ethnicity that is important. Rather it is His virtue and qualities that we are to be concerned with.

So how does Jesus fit into this picture? In 1Samuel 4-5 it is recorded that Israel lost the Ark of the Lord to the Philistines.

But the Philistines found that possession of the Ask brought them great misery instead of the power that they expected from it. So in 1Samuel 7 they returned it to Israel.

Then, in 1Samuel 7:5 the prophet Samuel ordered Israel to gather at Mizpah where he would make an offering to God. And while he was offering up a lamb the Philistines were gathered against Israel again. But the Lord thundered against the Philistines and Israel pursued them and smote them. Then, in verse 12, Samuel set up a stone for memorial and called it Ebenezer.

So the record shows that the Philistines were defeated at Mizpah with the help of the Lord, and an Ebenezer, literally "a stone of help," was set up to commemorate the victory.

Now, there are a couple of very significant things about this place Mizpah and to see what they are we have to go back to the book of Genesis.

We pick up the story where Laban catches up with Jacob and demands that Jacob returns all he has to Laban.

Genesis 31:43-52
"*And Laban answered and said unto Jacob, These daughters are my daughters, and these children are my children, and these cattle are my cattle, and all that thou seest is mine: and what can I do this day unto these my daughters, or unto their children which they have born?*

Now therefore come thou, let us make a covenant, I and thou; and let it be for a witness between me and thee.

And Jacob took a stone, and set it up for a pillar.

And Jacob said unto his brethren, Gather stones; and they took stones, and made an heap: and they did eat there upon the heap.

*And Laban called it **Jegar-sahadutha**: but Jacob called it **Galeed**.*

*And Laban said, This heap is a witness between me and thee this day. Therefore was the name of it called **Galeed**;*

*And **Mizpah**; for he said, The LORD watch between me and thee, when we are absent one from another.*

If thou shalt afflict my daughters, or if thou shalt take other wives beside my daughters, no man is with us; see, God is witness betwixt me and thee.

And Laban said to Jacob, Behold this heap, and behold this pillar, which I have cast betwixt me and thee;

This heap be witness, and this pillar be witness, that I will not pass over this heap to thee, and that thou shalt not pass over this heap and this pillar unto me, for harm."

In verse 47 Laban called it Sahadutha, which means "to gather a testimony or witness", but Jacob called it Galeed. Both mean "witness" although Galeed carries with it the sense of a spring of water.

In verses 48 and 49 Laban said, "This heap is a witness between you and me this day." Therefore its name was called Galeed, also Mizpah (a watch tower), because he said, "May the LORD watch between you and me when we are absent one from another.

In verse 52 Laban said to Jacob, "This heap is a witness, and this pillar is a witness that I will not pass beyond this heap to you, and you will not pass beyond this heap and this pillar to me, for harm. A stone had been placed between Jacob and Laban to keep them apart.

We know that Laban displays many of the characteristics of Satan while we saw that Genesis 25:27 declares Jacob to be a "tam" (complete or mature) man. We might say that in these two men we find a representation of the Devil on the one hand and a man under regeneration of the Holy Spirit on the other.

So here in Genesis 31 we see in Jacob a representation of the regenerated man separated from the world system. And as in the case of Jacob and Laban, or Israel and Philistia, there is only one thing that stands between them: The Blood and Testimony of Jesus of Nazareth, the Stone of God's Help, the Rock of our Salvation, Christ our Ebenezer.

Jesus of Nazareth is the One who stands between the believer, sin, death and the Devil.

1 Pet 2:6-9
"Wherefore also it is contained in the scripture, Behold, I lay in Sion a chief corner stone, elect, precious: and he that believeth on him shall not be confounded.

Unto you therefore which believe he is precious: but unto them which be disobedient, the stone which the builders disallowed, the same is made the head of the corner,

And a stone of stumbling, and a rock of offence, even to them which stumble at the word, being disobedient: whereunto also they were appointed.

But ye are a chosen generation, a royal priesthood, an holy nation, a peculiar people; that ye should shew forth the praises of him who hath called you out of darkness into his marvellous light ..."

"On Christ the solid Rock I stand, all other ground is sinking sand; all other ground is sinking sand."[5]

---

5   Solid Rock, Edward Mote, *circa* 1834

To Old Testament saints the Ebenezer was a stone of remembrance, a memorial to God's help. But the Ebenezer was a prophecy in stone that looked forward to the Rock that would save all who believe.

Is it just coincidence that Mizpah, the place of the memorial, is Hebrew for "waiting" and "peering into the distance?" This Stone of Help was more than a memorial – it faces in two directions – it anticipated the future as well as recalling the past.

Jacob placed a stone in Mizpah and they called it "Galeed" (testimony)

Samuel placed a stone in Mizpah and they called it "Ebenezer" (Rock of Help)

But God placed a stone in Bethlehem and called Him Jesus (Savior)

Chapter 13

RECOVERING WHAT WAS LOST

Romans 5:9-11

"Much more then, being now justified by his blood, we shall be saved from wrath through him.

For if, when we were enemies, we were reconciled to God by the death of his Son, much more, being reconciled, we shall be saved by his life.

And not only so, but we also joy in God through our Lord Jesus Christ, by whom we have now received the atonement."

Layer upon layer the Bible records events that proclaim the same message: That God gave the gift of life to man, man lost it, and God recovered it for him.

In 2 Kings Chapter 6 we find another of the many events illustrating this point. Here, in seven short verses, we find an obscure little incident that is traditionally taught as nothing more than the miracle of the floating ax head.

2 Kings 6:1-7

"And the sons of the prophets said unto Elisha, Behold now, the place where we dwell with thee is too strait for us.

Let us go, we pray thee, unto Jordan, and take thence every man a beam, and let us make us a place there, where we may dwell. And he answered, Go ye.

And one said, Be content, I pray thee, and go with thy servants. And he answered, I will go.

So he went with them. And when they came to Jordan, they cut down wood.

But as one was felling a beam, the axe head fell into the water: and he cried, and said, Alas, master! for it was borrowed.

And the man of God said, Where fell it? And he shewed him the place. And he cut down a stick, and cast it in thither; and the iron did swim.

Therefore said he, Take it up to thee. And he put out his hand, and took it."

The first thing to notice is that this section of the Scriptures is truly a non sequitur; that is, it appears to have nothing to do with anything that precedes it or follows it. It is an apple placed in the midst of oranges and I believe that it could have been made the smallest chapter in the Bible.

Disconnected ideas are not uncommon in the sacred writings of the many religions of the world. But what is unique to the Bible is that although an idea can be disconnected from the surrounding text, it is always in complete harmony with the basic theme or meta-narrative of the Word of God. That theme, as already stated, is that what God gave, man lost; and it could only be recovered by God. Keep that theme in mind as we explore this marvelous happening.

Here is an object lesson for the spiritually aware. Not just the miracle of an ax head floating but the greater miracle of God's promised salvation. Here is yet another illustration of a spiritual message residing within a historical event.

If we look beneath the surface of the text we will find all the ingredients that God has placed there for our encouragement. Perhaps we can see here man's plight in a fallen world and a desire for the return of a lost paradise.

In the first verse we find that a certain group called the sons of the prophets complained to the man of God that their present habitation is a tribulation to them. (The word translated "strait" is the Hebrew word "tsar", and it carries the sense of distress, trouble, or adversity.)

So they ask the prophet Elisha if it would be alright to relocate to the Jordan River where they can build a better place for themselves. Elisha simply says, "Go." Then one in the group begs the man of God to accompany them on their enterprise. Elisha simply says, "OKay."

When they get to the Jordan, construction begins and we can assume that all is proceeding as planned. But suddenly all the activity is interrupted by a single event: An ax head has been lost. It is imperative that it be recovered because it was borrowed.

What makes this such an important event that the construction should be interrupted by it? And what does it matter that it was borrowed? Can it not simply be replaced? Such questions aren't asked by Elisha. He only asks, "Where did you lose it?"

When Elisha was shown the place, he took a stick of wood and threw it into the water where the ax head had fallen. Then a miracle occurred; the ax head floated to the surface and the grateful man retrieved it from the water.

Now let's go beyond the traditional interpretation and apply a fresh hermeneutic to what God has placed here for our encouragement.

First of all it is generally accepted that the title "sons of the prophets" was given to the students in Israel's school of the prophets. It should also be noted that the prophet Elisha is a prefigure or type of the Lord Jesus.

When the sons of the prophets complain that their present habitation is an affliction and they want to go to a better place, they might be describing their fallen condition in metaphor. The Adamic curse is certainly a "strait" place. And it is certainly the heartfelt desire of man to rise above the privations and limitations of this fallen world.

It is in the nature of man to try to improve his conditions in his own strength and without any interference from God. Remember the Tower of Babel?

So they ask Elisha to accompany them to a place where they will build for themselves a more suitable habitation. Notice that they don't ask the man of God to build it for them.

As they requested, the man of God graciously goes with them. So often we invite God into our plans but exclude Him from their construction. In this case the builders are not qualified to improve on their conditions but that doesn't stop them from trying.

So they begin construction at the Jordan River. Now remember that the word "Jordan" means to "descend" or "fall". So beneath the surface we find that they are trying to improve their condition by building on the same cursed ground that is responsible for their plight. The message here is that any attempt of fallen man to save himself with ritual, or ceremony, or good works will never succeed.

Now while they are trying to build a better place for themselves, one of the workers loses an ax head in the waters of the Jordan. Here's where the symbols get difficult to follow without a strong understanding of the way that God uses words to communicate His mysteries.

The Hebrew word translated "ax head", is the word "bar-zel". Sometimes translated "iron", it is derived from a root that literally means "to pierce".

At this point let me say a little about the original language that the Bible was written in. The Old Testament is translated from Hebrew and the New Testament comes to us from Greek. Both of these languages stimulate imagery in the mind of the reader. That is to say, the words convey ideas as pictures.

In other words, a name in English is little more than a label and as such might have absolutely nothing to do with who or what is named. However, in the Hebrew or the Greek a name relates to a quality or characteristic of the one so named.

Throughout the Scriptures the names of people and places tell us so much more about who and what they are than merely labeling them for identification. So when a Hebrew saw the word "bar-zel" he would have thought of it according to its function, which is to "pierce" wood.

What makes this so significant is the fact that the idea of piercing occupies such a prominent place in the entire Canon of Scripture. It is associated again and again with Jesus and His Crucifixion. His hands and feet were pierced by nails. His head was pierced by thorns. And His side was pierced by a Roman spear.

In the loss of the ax head in the waters of the Jordan we can see a picture of 2 Cor 5:21 which says that, *"… he hath made him to be sin for us, who knew no sin; that we might be made the righteousness of God in him."*

The One who was pierced for our transgressions was thrown into the Fall ("Adamic curse") that He may be a partaker of our fallen condition and so overcome it. As it says in Hebrews 2:14, *"Forasmuch then as the children are partakers of flesh and blood, he also himself likewise took part of the same; that through death he might destroy him that had the power of death, that is, the devil …"*

As the ax head falls into the water, the man cries out to the prophet, "Alas Master, it was borrowed". I find it fascinating that the word translated "alas" actually means, "love" or "affection". This shows that the relationship between the man who lost the ax head and Elisha is one of closeness.

And what about the statement; "It was borrowed"?

To understand that we have to go back to Genesis 2:7, where, *"… the LORD God formed man of the dust of the ground, and breathed into his nostrils the breath of life; and man became a living soul."*

The Bible makes it clear that life is from God. And as it says in Eccl 12:7, *"Then shall the dust return to the earth as it was: and the spirit shall return unto God who gave it."*

Life is from God and it is borrowed. Jesus gave it back to God on the Cross and God gave it back to Him in eternity. So, in simple terms, it means that when you surrender your life to God, He will give it back to you in eternity. Jesus declares in Mark 8:35, *"For whosoever will save his life shall lose it; but whosoever shall lose his life for my sake and the gospel's, the same shall save it."*

Then the prophet took a tree (Heb. Ets: wood) and threw it into the waters of the Jordan. In doing this he was symbolically applying the Cross of Christ to the Adamic curse. The wood that Jesus was hung on (also called a "tree") was the vehicle that God used to atone for the sin of the world. As soon as the tree was thrown into the Jordan (a picture of the Cross being applied to the Fall) the miracle occurred and the Fall was overcome by the Piercing. Then it was recovered for the one who had lost it.

Our translations read that the ax head ("piercing") swam or floated. But the original Hebrew word should be translated "overflowed or overcame".

What a picture we see here of the recovery of lost souls; and of lost paradise restored by the only One who could accomplish it.

In this brief account we can see the Savior who threw Himself into the deep waters of human suffering in order to overcome the condition and recover all that had been lost by Adam.

Jesus produced many miracles that are a source of delight and wonder to us all. But they were mostly done to endorse His Divine authority and identify Him as Messiah. Behind His miraculous healings can be found His higher purpose: Recovering lost souls to the Father.

What a merciful God we serve. He has not left us orphans, lost and alone, without hope. But he has pursued us even into the very curse that separated us from Him, and by His sacrifice has gloriously overcome it. He has rescued us from the dominion of darkness and brought us into His Kingdom of Light. Truly, as the Apostle writes in 1Timothy 3:16, *"And without controversy great is the mystery of godliness: God was manifest in the flesh, justified in the Spirit, seen of angels, preached unto the Gentiles, believed on in the world, received up into glory."*

Chapter 14

GOD SENT A WORM

Jonah 4:6-7
And the LORD God prepared a gourd, and made it to come up over Jonah, that it might be a shadow over his head, to deliver him from his grief. So Jonah was exceeding glad of the gourd. But God prepared a worm when the morning rose the next day, and it smote the gourd that it withered.

In this living parable God tells us how He stepped out of eternity and took on the dual nature of man and God. As Jesus of Nazareth He would exposed Himself to the Adamic curse and overcome it for the sake of fallen man.

We begin by looking at the meaning of the names of the principals in the above narrative. Jonah, which means "dove", was the son of Amittai, which comes from a root that means "stability and truth".

Considering that the dove is a well established symbol of peace and was the likeness of what descended on Jesus at His baptism, the logical inference is that Jonah actually represents the Son of God.

The Book of Jonah begins with Jonah being instructed by the Word of the Lord to go to Nineveh and warn them of the consequences of their wickedness.

According to Jones' Dictionary Of Old Testament Proper Names,[6] Nineveh means, the "habitation of the offspring". So in the first two verses of this book we may see the Lord in hypostatic union coming into the world to give warning of judgment to Adam's offspring.

The dual nature or identity represented in Jonah is further shown as the story continues and he shows his reluctance to obey the Word of the Lord by boarding a ship and fleeing in the opposite direction to Tarshish. The same reluctance is seen in the Lord Jesus as He struggles with His human fear in Gethsemane.

Matthew 26:39

"And he went a little farther, and fell on his face, and prayed, saying, O my Father, if it be possible, let this cup pass from me: nevertheless not as I will, but as thou wilt."

Jonah's rebellion resulted in a tremendous storm and the ship and crew were in danger of sinking. While the crew was panicking Jonah was down inside the ship sleeping. He was aroused by the captain and taken up on deck where they cast lots to see who was responsible for this great storm. The lot fell to Jonah.

There is an incident from the Gospels that mirrors this part of the account:

Matthew 8:23-24

"And when he was entered into a ship, his disciples followed him. And, behold, there arose a great tempest in the sea, insomuch that the ship was covered with the waves: but he was asleep."

---

6 Jones' Dictionary Of Old Testament Proper Names. Page 277.

Jonah then told the crew that he was responsible for the storm and that they must throw him into the sea. At this point Jonah is representative of Adam's self- righteousness which is responsible for the Fall. The storm, or Fall, can only be overcome by throwing Jonah into the sea; a picture of the incarnation and Cross of Christ.

The men were afraid to do as Jonah said and wanted to save themselves by their own strength. They tried to row Jonah to shore but they found that the storm was too great for them. So they did as Jonah said and cast him into the sea and the storm immediately ceased.

Again, this part of the account can be seen mirrored in the Gospel:

Matthew 27:24-25
"When Pilate saw that he could prevail nothing, but that rather a tumult was made, he took water, and washed his hands before the multitude, saying, I am innocent of the blood of this just person: see ye to it. Then answered all the people, and said, His blood be on us, and on our children."

The whole second chapter speaks of the Passion of Christ. This is why Jesus compares His death and resurrection to Jonah's three days and three nights in the belly of the whale.

Matthew 12:40
"For as Jonas was three days and three nights in the whale's belly; so shall the Son of man be three days and three nights in the heart of the earth."

In the third chapter Nineveh received Jonah's warning and they were saved from destruction. The obvious message here is that repentance leads to salvation.

Mark 1:4
"John did baptize in the wilderness, and preach the baptism of repentance for the remission of sins."

Being that memory fades and human nature is fickle, it is no surprise that Nineveh did eventually return to their wicked ways and suffered the appropriate consequences. So it is with all of humankind apart from the salvation offered by God in Jesus of Nazareth.

The fourth chapter brings us to the climax of the Gospel in prophecy. Jonah was unhappy with God's forgiveness of such a wicked people and insisted that they must be punished. Human nature demands an eye for an eye but Divine justice only requires repentance and the acceptance of the substitutionary payment made by Jesus on the Cross.

Jonah separated himself from Nineveh and built for himself a shelter so that he could sit in the shade and brood over the city. He begged God to take his life from him for he said it is better for him to die than to live. Several Messianic symbols are to be seen in these passages:

John 10:17-18
"Therefore doth my Father love me, because I lay down my life, that I might take it again. No man taketh it from me, but I lay it down of myself. I have power to lay it down, and I have power to take it again. This commandment have I received of my Father."

Now while Jonah was sitting in the shade of the shelter built with his own hands, God prepared a gourd to be a shadow over Jonah's head to deliver him from his grief. This pleased Jonah but the following day God prepared a worm to strike the gourd and Jonah's head was fully exposed to the heat of the sun.

The first thing to notice in these last passages is that Jonah, representing carnal man, seeks to shield himself from the righteousness of God by the works of his own hands. But there is a sickness carried over from Adam's transgression. This sickness is presented as a gourd (from the Hebrew "qiygayown"), which literally means "nauseous" and comes from a root that means "to vomit". On a different level the gourd represents the Law that God gave to show man his sin and need of a Savior.

The worm that God sent on the following day to strike the gourd and fulfill the Law, was the "towla". The towla was known as the "scarlet" or "crimson" worm because its crushed body produced the red dye that colors the garments worn by royalty.

The Brown-Driver-Briggs lexicon presents an interesting description of the towla:-

"When the female of the scarlet worm species is ready to give birth to her young, she attaches her body to the trunk of a tree, fixing herself so firmly and permanently that she never leaves again. The eggs deposited beneath her body are thus protected until the larvae are hatched and able to enter their own life cycle.
"When the mother dies, the crimson fluid stains her body and the surrounding wood. From the dead bodies of such female

scarlet worms, the commercial scarlet dyes of antiquity [the color of royalty] were extracted." [7]

What a picture this gives of Christ, dying on the tree, shedding His precious blood that He might "bring many sons unto glory" (Heb. 2:10)! He died for us, that we might live through Him!"

In the worm we have a type of Christ who came to eat the gourd: that is, to take the sickness of the Adamic curse into Himself, into His own body, to satisfy the Law, and bring Divine healing to fallen man.

2 Cor 5:21
"For he hath made him to be sin for us, who knew no sin; that we might be made the righteousness of God in him."

Once again, in this historical account of Jonah and the worm God has left us the promise of divine reconciliation as given in the third chapter of Genesis. Because of Jesus of Nazareth all who believe are clothed in the crimson garments of royalty dyed with the blood of God's own Towla. (Jesus Christ)

It is all too glorious for human comprehension. And I find myself joining with the Apostle Paul in:

Rom 11:33-36
"O the depth of the riches both of the wisdom and knowledge of God! how unsearchable are his judgments, and his ways past finding out!

For who hath known the mind of the Lord? or who hath been his counsellor?

---

7   The Biblical Basis for Modern Science. Page 73.

Or who hath first given to him, and it shall be recompensed unto him again?

For of him, and through him, and to him, are all things: to whom be glory for ever."

Amen.

Chapter 15

CLEAN AND UNCLEAN

Mark 7:14-20

"And when he had called all the people unto him, he said unto them, 'Hearken unto me every one of you, and understand:

There is nothing from without a man, that entering into him can defile him: but the things which come out of him, those are they that defile the man.

If any man have ears to hear, let him hear.

And when he was entered into the house from the people, his disciples asked him concerning the parable.

And he saith unto them, Are ye so without understanding also? Do ye not perceive, that whatsoever thing from without entereth into the man, it cannot defile him;

Because it entereth not into his heart, but into the belly, and goeth out into the draught, purging all meats?

And he said, That which cometh out of the man, that defileth the man.'"

This was a totally new concept for the Jews. And a difficult one to grasp for a people who had 1,500 years of tradition that strictly regulated what they put in their mouths to eat.

When Jesus said, "Hear and understand", He knew that the traditions had taught the people their dietary customs but they hadn't seen the reason behind those customs. At this point

Jesus wasn't actually explaining to them what the reasons were; rather He was encouraging them to think about what they had always blindly adhered to.

He told them that food and drink have no power to affect a man's moral life. The Apostle Paul continued to treat this subject in his letter to the Corinthians.

1 Cor 8:8
"… food does not commend us to God; for neither if we eat are we the better, nor if we do not eat are we the worse."

What a shock this must have been for the Jews. How difficult do you suppose it was for them to deny these teachings, these practices that had been handed down from Moses himself? Even to this day the Jews continue to observe the Levitical dietary laws without understanding what they truly represent. To them it is merely a matter of being Jewish. But Paul said that it went way beyond being Jewish.

As followers of Jesus we all believe that He is the fulfillment of the Levitical food laws. But have you ever wondered in what way He is their fulfillment? What is the significance of the Levitical ordinances regarding clean and unclean foods? It may seem a strange place to start, but for reasons that I hope will become clear as we go along, we begin our study in eternity past.

The following explanation will not answer every question that may arise. In fact, in all likelihood it will generate a few questions. But its purpose is to give an overview that is consistent with the data that is available to us from the Scriptures.

According to the Bible, God created the heavens and the earth. It is to be assumed that all was well in the universe at that time because God is perfect and He can only create according to who and what He is.

The Scriptures tell us that God is good and in James 1:17 we are told that He is the Father of lights in whom there is no changing. That means that God is totally reliable because He is without caprice. He is never double minded. And He only does what is good and what is right. It follows then that God's creation was initially good.

As we have already seen, it remained unblemished until a cherub named Lucifer challenged God's position and coveted it for himself. This resulted in a war of cosmic proportions. Where there had been unity in the Host of heaven, there was now division and opposition to the Will of God.

When Lucifer opposed God death entered into His perfect creation and death brought with it decay. Through Adam's transgression, death and decay entered man and defiled his world.

Then the flood came and cleaned everything. But God preserved Noah and his family and every creature that Noah had taken aboard the Ark. Why do you suppose God told Noah to take the creeping things on the Ark with him? Surely the world would be a better place without flies and cockroaches and all the other pests that we must share the world with now.

Well, remember that the world after the flood was still a fallen world full of death and decay. Death produces refuse. And since everything in the world is subject to death, it is necessary that there be a cleanup crew to keep the place livable.

Your local garbage collector may pick up your trash, but they are not the ones responsible for its breakdown and return to the natural elements. That is the job of the agents of decay. It has been said that without the carrion eating animals and the insects and bacteria, we would be knee deep in garbage in just a few months. Here, I believe, is the beginning of understanding.

The Lord told the Hebrews not to eat anything that He declared to be unclean. So how did they differ from what is declared to be clean and fit to eat? As we shall see, they are all agents of decay.

First of all, it can be seen from the Scriptures that the animals that could be used for food were animals that have a split hoof and chew their cud. They represent the people who would meditate on the Word of God, as represented in chewing the cud, and would walk another path. This is a picture of a changed life or repentance signified by the leaving of a split track in their walk.

The clean animal must fulfill both requirements of chewing the cud and having a split hoof. The pig for example, declared to be an unclean animal, has a split hoof but doesn't chew the cud. Symbolically this refers to one who is willing to change his walk (lifestyle) but will not adopt Divine viewpoint. He is the one who will appear to accept God's Word as truth but soon returns to his former life just as the pig returns to the mire.

Many Christians today believe that pork is prohibited for reasons of health. But the real reason is not what the pig has in its flesh but rather what it represents in the spiritual sense.

2 Peter 2:22
"Of them the proverbs are true: 'A dog returns to its vomit,' and, 'A sow that is washed goes back to her wallowing in the mud.'"

Even the Jews know that the prohibition of pork has nothing to do with health. On page 87 of *The Jewish Book Of Why*,[8] Rabbi Kolatch, says, *"… the purpose of the dietary laws was to bring holiness and unity to the Jewish people, not good health."*

Little does he realize the profound truth in that statement; holiness and unity can only come to any people through the reality that these laws fore-shadowed.

Col 2:16-17
Let no man therefore judge you in meat, or in drink, or in respect of an holyday, or of the new moon, or of the sabbath days: Which are a shadow of things to come; but the body is of Christ.

Now when we look at the pig and the other unacceptable animals we can see that they represent all those people who reject Godliness in favor of their own world view or lifestyle. By opposing God they make themselves, in type, agents of decay because they align themselves with the Lord of decay – Beelzebub, the Devil.

In **1Cor 5:11** the Apostle Paul instructs the Christian not to even eat with one who claims to be a brother in the Lord but lives an immoral life. Why? Because eating together denotes acceptance. And for that reason the Hebrews where to eat

---

8 The Jewish Book Of Why c1981 by Alfred J. kolatch. Page 87

differently from the nations. In this way they would remain separate from their neighbors and maintain the line by which the Messiah would come.

In addition to unclean animals, God prohibited the eating of all creeping things with the exception of the grasshopper and his relatives which only eat vegetation. This was because the other insects are all agents of decay in that they eat carrion or other insects; to eat them would symbolize joining with them in their purpose which is to return things to the earth.

So, simple terms, it can be shown that the Levitical food laws had nothing to do with health. The Apostle Paul makes that clear in his letter to Timothy in regard to eating and drinking.

1 Tim 4:4
"For everything God created is good, and nothing is to be rejected if it is received with thanksgiving ..."

In the Scriptures the eating of clean foods represented the intake and assimilation of the Word of God which feeds and cleanses the soul. The Bible declares that Jesus is the Word of God in the flesh. He is the result of a life that is sustained by Godliness. Jesus fulfills the purpose of the Levitical food laws.

It's like that old adage, "You are what you eat", or you become what you align yourself with. Our choices are life or death, law or grace, order or chaos. This is not to say that we are not to associate with the unbeliever as it did mean for the Hebrew. Paul addressed this in his first letter to the Corinthians.

1 Cor 5:9-13

I wrote unto you in an epistle not to company with fornicators:

Extortioners, or with idolaters; for then must ye needs go out of the world.

But now I have written unto you not to keep company, if any man that is called a brother be a fornicator, or covetous, or an idolater, or a railer, or a drunkard, or an extortioner; with such an one no not to eat.

For what have I to do to judge them also that are without? do not ye judge them that are within?

But them that are without God judgeth. Therefore put away from among yourselves that wicked person.

The message is simple. God's people are to avoid ungodliness, which ends in decay, and seek the righteousness that leads to life. Such righteousness is only found in the Lord Jesus and those who follow Him.

Hebrews 13:9

"Do not be carried away by all kinds of strange teachings. It is good for our hearts to be strengthened by grace, not by ceremonial foods, which are of no value to those who eat them."

Chapter 16

THE AWESOME POWER OF PEACE

1Kings 19:11
"And he said, Go forth, and stand upon the mount before the LORD. And, behold, the LORD passed by, and a great and strong wind rent the mountains, and brake in pieces the rocks before the LORD; but the LORD was not in the wind: and after the wind an earthquake; but the LORD was not in the earthquake.."

Some time ago I realized that there is a strange dichotomy in our perception of the character of God. On the one hand He is an agent of violence who can destroy anything He chooses to, and on the other He is telling us that He loves us with an everlasting love, shielding us from a ruthless enemy bent on our destruction.

It would seem that the same Bible that presents an angry and destructive God in the Old Testament presents a loving and forgiving one in the New Testament. For this reason many assume that in the Old Testament God was in the process of growing into the more mature being that is portrayed in the New Testament.

This confusion about the nature of God has caused people to be ambivalent towards Him. Many see a God with two faces; one that blesses and one that curses. However, we are assured that God is perfect and as such is good and cannot change. He does not change because perfection is an absolute. There is no such thing as a degree of perfection.

James 1:17
"Every good gift and every perfect gift is from above, and cometh down from the Father of lights, with whom is no variableness, neither shadow of turning."

It is in the nature of man to be impressed with strength, and often strength is equated with violence. Just think of how the movie industry has capitalized on this with their special effects specialists constantly blowing things up to the delight of the audience. We have, in our nature, the mistaken idea that real power is in the ability to overcome any obstacle by force.

Consider also how the insurance industry designates any form of natural violence, such as hurricanes, tornados, earthquakes, and all related phenomena, as ACTS OF GOD. This shows a woeful ignorance of the true nature of our wonderful and loving Creator.

The traditional view of God as the mover of mountains and the great enforcer of His commandments is well established. But perhaps there is a better understanding of God's character to be found in His manifestation as the PRINCE OF PEACE.

The prophet Elijah learned something about this when he was running from Jezebel and ended up in a cave in Horeb, the mountain of the Law. We begin the story as Elijah challenges the prophets of Baal to prove the power of their gods.

1Kings 18:25-40

"And Elijah said unto the prophets of Baal, Choose you one bullock for yourselves, and dress it first; for ye are many; and call on the name of your gods, but put no fire under.

And they took the bullock which was given them, and they dressed it, and called on the name of Baal from morning even until noon, saying, O Baal, hear us. But there was no voice, nor any that answered. And they leaped upon the altar which was made.

And it came to pass at noon, that Elijah mocked them, and said, Cry aloud: for he is a god; either he is talking, or he is pursuing, or he is in a journey, or peradventure he sleepeth, and must be awaked.

And they cried aloud, and cut themselves after their manner with knives and lancets, till the blood gushed out upon them.

And it came to pass, when midday was past, and they prophesied until the time of the offering of the evening sacrifice, that there was neither voice, nor any to answer, nor any that regarded.

And Elijah said unto all the people, Come near unto me. And all the people came near unto him. And he repaired the altar of the LORD that was broken down.

And Elijah took twelve stones, according to the number of the tribes of the sons of Jacob, unto whom the word of the LORD came, saying, Israel shall be thy name:

And with the stones he built an altar in the name of the LORD: and he made a trench about the altar, as great as would contain two measures of seed.

And he put the wood in order, and cut the bullock in pieces, and laid him on the wood, and said, Fill four barrels with water, and pour it on the burnt sacrifice, and on the wood.

And he said, Do it the second time. And they did it the second time. And he said, Do it the third time. And they did it the third time.

And the water ran round about the altar; and he filled the trench also with water.

And it came to pass at the time of the offering of the evening sacrifice, that Elijah the prophet came near, and said, LORD God of Abraham, Isaac, and of Israel, let it be known this day that thou art God in Israel, and that I am thy servant, and that I have done all these things at thy word.

Hear me, O LORD, hear me, that this people may know that thou art the LORD God, and that thou hast turned their heart back again.

Then the fire of the LORD fell, and consumed the burnt sacrifice, and the wood, and the stones, and the dust, and licked up the water that was in the trench.

And when all the people saw it, they fell on their faces: and they said, The LORD, he is the God; the LORD, he is the God.

And Elijah said unto them, Take the prophets of Baal; let not one of them escape. And they took them: and Elijah brought them down to the brook Kishon, and slew them there."

What a picture of raw power this incident presents. Who isn't reminded of the mighty God who visited the plagues on the arrogant house of Pharaoh? Or the parting of the Red Sea into which the implacable Egyptians rode to their doom?

Doesn't this speak of the powerful God who delivered Israel's enemies into their hands over and over again? And who brought disaster into the house of Israel after she had fallen into disobedience and carnal decadence?

Again, most surely it is in our nature to be impressed and encouraged by the notion of such astounding and irresistible power. It gives us great comfort and security to know that we are friends with the biggest, baddest guy on the block.

But when the story continues in the next chapter we might see things from a different angle. We resume the story as Elijah flees Jezebel's anger for killing her prophets and enters a cave in Mount Horeb, the mountain of the Law.

1 Kings 19:9-12

"And he came thither unto a cave, and lodged there; and, behold, the word of the LORD came to him, and he said unto him, What doest thou here, Elijah?

And he said, I have been very jealous for the LORD God of hosts: for the children of Israel have forsaken thy covenant, thrown down thine altars, and slain thy prophets with the sword; and I, even I only, am left; and they seek my life, to take it away.

And he said, Go forth, and stand upon the mount before the LORD. And, behold, the LORD passed by, and a great and strong wind rent the mountains, and brake in pieces the rocks before the LORD; but the LORD was not in the wind: and after the wind an earthquake; but the LORD was not in the earthquake:

And after the earthquake a fire; but the LORD was not in the fire: and after the fire a still small voice."

Let's look again at Elijah's adventure and see if it might not be understood a little differently and more in keeping with the Father revealed in the personality and character of Jesus of Nazareth.

At Mt. Horeb, the place of the giving of the Law, Elijah entered a cave. While he was in the cave the Word of the Lord came to Elijah and asked him, "What are you doing here Elijah?" Elijah answered, "I alone have been defending God's honor and now my life is in danger."

God then proceeded to teach Elijah an important lesson. He told Elijah to "Go stand on the mountain before the Lord;"

113

this is tantamount to God saying, "Stand on My Truth and hear Me."

As Elijah stood on the mountain we read that the Lord passed by and a great strong wind tore the mountains and broke the rocks into pieces. After the wind there was an earthquake. And after the earthquake there was fire. What an impressive demonstration of God's awesome power was shown to Elijah. The only problem is that in each case the Lord said that He was not in any of them.

Finally, after the demonstration, Elijah could hear the voice of God. He had moved into relationship with God. This must always be the order of sanctification: First the Word, then the abandoning of the old for the new, then the refinement of the character. At the end of the process God waits with open arms like the Father receiving His prodigal son.

Was God in the storm? Was He in the earthquake? Was He in the fire? Certainly we can find places that seem to say He is in all those things. But God tells us that He is not in any of them, and He cannot lie. So what is the solution to this mystery?

Perhaps we can find some clues in God's own Word.

Isaiah 54:16
"Behold, I have created the smith that bloweth the coals in the fire, and that bringeth forth an instrument for his work; and I have created the waster to destroy."

Here is another clue from the New Testament:

John 10:10

"The thief cometh not, but for to steal, and to kill, and to destroy: I am come that they might have life, and that they might have it more abundantly.

When we read the Scriptures carefully we can see that God is not the author of confusion (1Cor 14:33), neither is He the source of violence or destruction as we can see in the following example from the Exodus record.

Exodus 12:23

"For the LORD will pass through to smite the Egyptians; and when he seeth the blood upon the lintel, and on the two side posts, the LORD will pass over the door, and will not suffer the destroyer to come in unto your houses to smite you."

There are many verses that show that God's nature is to shield us from harm. When the Enemy moves to take advantage of us, as is his nature, it is God who sets limits on how far he can go. This is made clear in the first chapter of the Book of Job.

Job 1:12

"And the LORD said unto Satan, Behold, all that he hath is in thy power; only upon himself put not forth thine hand. So Satan went forth from the presence of the LORD."

Elijah leaned that God is not in the wind, the earthquake, or the fire. So what is God telling us in this account? As we have already seen, God paints pictures for us with His words. And the picture that He has painted here might be interpreted in this way:

1. The wind is to break the old established teachings and world view.

2. The earthquake is symbolic of reordering the broken pieces of the former life and viewpoint.
3. The fire is symbolic of refinement as the dross is separated from what is acceptable to a holy God.

The violence that some would attribute to God is actually inherent in the refining process. God is that gentle, kind, faithful, compassionate, and patient presence that sustains and encourages us throughout our struggles within a fallen world and faithfully completes the good work that He starts in us.

Understand that it is not God who corrupted this universe and sent it on its tormented course toward destruction. Rather, He is a loving, caring God who has reached into the chaos of this dying world and built the only avenue of escape from a fate too hideous to comprehend. And He did all it at His own expense.

So, natural storms and seismic activity are all consequences of the Fall and the Adamic curse. The power of God is not the cause of these destructive forces. Rather the power of God is to the stilling of them.

Notice how the storm that threatened the disciples of Jesus on the sea of Galilee was instantly calmed with a few simple words.

Mark 4:38-39
"And he was in the hinder part of the ship, asleep on a pillow: and they awake him, and say unto him, Master, carest thou not that we perish? And he arose, and rebuked the wind, and said unto the sea, Peace, be still. And the wind ceased, and there was a great calm."

The question here is, where is the greatest power? Is it in the storm or is it in the stilling of the storm? Let's see God as He is revealed through Jesus, the Prince of Peace.

Notice how Jesus dealt with dangers and demons. He didn't rave and bluster at the storm or the demons that were tormenting people. He simply overpowered them with His peace. Look at what the people said about Jesus when He delivered a man possessed by evil spirits.

Mark 1:27:
Then they were all amazed, so that they questioned among themselves, saying, "What is this? What new doctrine is this? For with authority He commands even the unclean spirits, and they obey Him."

What is this peace that can paradoxically command demons and still the storm? What is this gentleness that can tame the violence of both nature and Satan? It is the absence of hostility. It is the presence of the virtues or strengths of God in the character of a life lived to His glory. It is the irresistible order that can be found in conformance to God's Holy Will. It is the Love of God that transforms the defective into perfection and the hideous into the beautiful.

And the peace of God is available to anybody who would trust Him and seek His Will in life; if we would offer ourselves as living sacrifices and defer our methods and attitudes to His methods and attitudes. Such is the replacement of human viewpoint with Divine viewpoint and human character with Divine Character.

As Elijah learned, **it starts with "hearing" the "Word" of God, and ends with entering into "relationship" with God.** The still, small voice of God is only heard after the Word of God takes up residence in the soul of the believer.

Israel could only know God as He seemed to be through the struggles and conflicts that were necessary to **protect the Messianic line** and assure His entry into the world. But we can know Him as He truly is through Jesus who is the fullness of the Godhead in bodily form (Col 2:9). It is for good reason that Jesus is called the Prince of Peace.

Isaiah 59:19
"… When the enemy shall come in like a flood, the Spirit of the LORD shall lift up a standard against him."

The Lord promises peace and victory over all the trials and storms of life to anybody who will put their trust in Him and put His Word in their heart.

Phil 4:6-7
"Be careful for nothing; but in every thing by prayer and supplication with thanksgiving let your requests be made known unto God. And the peace of God, which passeth all understanding, shall keep your hearts and minds through Christ Jesus."

So how do we answer God's question to Elijah? He asks, "What are you doing here Elijah? Are you killing all My enemies for Me with carnal anger and self-righteousness?" And "Where do you live Elijah? Is it in a world where strength is measured by the ability to knock things down and get your own way?"

In a very real way God asks the same questions of us. How do we manifest God's Will in our lives? Do we serve the Lord in ways that are inconsistent with His character? Or do we live in that Kingdom ruled by grace and compassion, kindness, goodness, patience and faithfulness? A place where there is victory through the awesome power of peace?

Chapter 17

JESUS WAS A CARPENTER

Some time ago, the telephone rang; I picked it up and found myself talking with a friend who was almost 200 miles away. I began to marvel at the instrument that enabled this miraculous feat, when suddenly I realized that the real miracle here was something we have come to take for granted even more than the telephone. I am speaking about language, communication, words.

Just think, by using words, without the benefit of gestures, eye contact, facial expressions, or the many other nuances of communication, we were able to exchange a wealth of both abstract and concrete information during our conversation.

Words have been called "the ultimate unit of meaning" because they cannot be divided further and remain whole. However, words, like people, have relatives who can contribute to their character and meaning. These relatives are called "roots".

The Greek language, which the New Testament was originally written in, makes extensive use of root derivatives. These "roots" can often help us to see deeper into the meaning of a word than a simple definition can. Take, for example, the Greek word for "carpenter." By simple definition this word gives us the meaning of "one who fashions things out of wood". A broader meaning is also contained in the word - that of an architect or builder in wood, stone or metal. But if we would dare to follow the cascade of meaning revealed by its relatives, the roots, we would make an exciting discovery.

The Greek word for "carpenter" is "tekton" - from which we get the English word "technology". Tekton means "a craftsman in wood" but its immediate root derivative is "timoria", which means *"vindication"* (justification against denial or censure) or "a *penalty*; a *punishment*".

Timoria, in turn, is derived from the root "timorio", which means "to *protect one's honor; to inflict a penalty*". The chain continues with the next root - "time", which means "*a value; something paid; a precious price*". The chain ends with the root "tino", which means "*to pay a price, as a penalty*".

What do any of these roots have to do with carpentry? And yet they are all part of the word for carpenter. Surely God has a profound message hidden within the simple word "carpenter." There are only two places in the New Testament where this word "carpenter" is used: Matthew 13:55 and Mark 6:3.

In Matthew there is an allusion to Jesus being the son of a carpenter (Joseph), while in Mark, Jesus Himself is referred to as a carpenter. Liberal theologians have noted here a discrepancy. They view the statement in Matthew as a denial of the virgin birth of Jesus by claiming that it plainly states that Joseph was the father of Jesus.

However, if we look at the meaning of the word "carpenter" and keep in mind the purpose or mission of Jesus as revealed in the New Testament, we will make an astounding discovery.

Carpenter was not just His profession, it was His commission; it was what He was appointed to do.

One can hardly read the related meanings of the word "carpenter" without being reminded of Jesus as the suffering servant whose purpose it was to atone for the sins of mankind. He alone could reunite man to God through an act of *vindication*, as He suffered the *penalty*, and *paid the price* that was rightfully ours, by dying in our place.

As we meditate on these amazing correlations, we turn our attention to the father who, Matthew tells us, is also a carpenter. Although Joseph was only the legal father of Jesus, when the people of Nazareth identified Jesus as "the carpenter's son," they were unwittingly affirming His Divine origin since, as the Gospels tell us, God Himself took on a physical body and came to be among men. Therefore, everything that is implied by the designation "carpenter" not only applies to Jesus but to God the Father, as well.

This presents the wonderful picture of a judge who, after pronouncing the sentence that is demanded by the law, strips himself of his robe of authority and presents himself to pay the imposed penalty as a substitute for the prisoner, for whom he cares deeply.

There is a final point to be made about the word "carpenter." It is a word that signifies a builder, an artisan, a creator or designer. Surely it is a wonderful thing to see the connection between this designation and John 1:1-5, which says, *"In the beginning was the Word, and the Word was with God, and the Word was God. The same was in the beginning with God. All things were made by him; and without him was not any thing made that was made. In him was life; and the life was the light of men. And the light shineth in darkness; and the darkness comprehended it not."*

God the Father and Creator of all things took on humanity in the person of Jesus of Nazareth as foretold by the prophets, and as such paid the penalty for sin (as imposed by Divine justice) in our place. Who would ever have thought that all this could by found hidden within the simple word "carpenter?"

Praise God.

Chapter 18

THE NAME OF GOD AS CREATOR

It is generally assumed that the name of God as Creator is "Elohiym". This is most likely because of the use of that Hebrew term in the first verse of the Bible and, in fact, throughout the first three chapters of the book of Genesis.

However, it is quite likely that there is a more appropriate name for God as Creator since the Hebrew word "Elohiym" is defined in Strong's Lexicon as "judges" or "magistrates." The designation "Elohiym" used in the first few chapters of the Bible might be more accurately referring to God in His judicial identity.

It must be remembered that the first verses of the Gospel of John state that it was the "Logos" that created all that there is. The Logos or Word is, of course, referring to the Lord Jesus Christ.

John 1:1-5
"In the beginning was the Word, and the Word was with God, and the Word was God. The same was in the beginning with God. All things were made by him; and without him was not any thing made that was made. In him was life; and the life was the light of men. And the light shineth in darkness; and the darkness comprehended it not."

There is, of course, only one true God, and the names of God are not referring to entirely different entities but are designations describing attributes or manifestations of the One Unique Entity that the English Bible calls "God".

Throughout the Scriptures, God is named according to the way He interacts with man or His creation. For example, in Exodus 15:26, God is called Yehovah Raphah – God as "Healer." Or, as in Genesis 22:14 God is called Yehovah Yireh – "God will be seen," or as is traditionally known – "God our provider." And the list goes on with Yehovah Nissi – "God our Banner;" Yehovah Shalom – "God our Peace;" or El Shaddai – "God Almighty." You get the idea.

A name of God that has been the source of much debate over the centuries is "Yahweh". Often written simply as YHVH, it is a transliteration of the four Hebrew letters with which God identified Himself to Moses in Exodus 3:14.

God's statement to Moses, "I AM that I AM" is referred to as the Tetragrammaton which is a word that means, "a word that is made up of four letters"; or perhaps it would be more accurate to say, "a word that is made up of four words".

These four Hebrew letters that make up the name Yahweh began as pictograms, a type of hieroglyphic, in the time of Moses. The four letters are Yod, Heh, Vav, and Heh. Or, if you prefer, Yodh, He, Waw, He.

Whatever the preference, each of the pictograms had a meaning:
1. The Yod represented a hand;
2. The Heh was a wind-door (window);
3. The Vav was a nail;
4. And the second Heh was also a wind- door or window.

The interesting thing about the Tetragrammaton is that although it is traditionally read as a group of letters, it might have originally been read as a group of words or symbols which made a statement.

If it is read as a group of letters it is commonly pronounced "Yahweh". However if it is read as a group of words or symbols it might take on a fascinating new meaning. Could it be that it is not just the sacred name of God, but a formula for Creation?

Consider the Yod, as a hand, expressing a desire or a cause – the hand reaches for what is desired. The Heh, as a wind-door, is a picture of what is seen on the other side of a wall – a scene or picture it you will.

The Vav, as a nail, is a fastener used to hold something together. The second Heh, also a wind-door or window, again presents a view of what is seen on the other side of a wall. In this ancient name of God we might see not only the Creator of all there is but also the method by which He accomplished it.

In theology God is known as the uncaused cause of everything there is – He is without beginning or end. In the Tetragrammaton we might see the Yod as God reaching for what He imagines or sees in the Heh or window of His divine mind. The Vav might be God the Son, Jesus fashioning the whole of Creation "ex-nihilo," that is out of nothing. And in the final Heh the entire universe springs into being.

Col 1:16
For by Him [Jesus] *were all things created, that are in heaven, and that are in earth, visible and invisible, whether they be thrones, or*

dominions, or principalities, or powers: all things were created by him, and for him..."

In simple terms Yahweh, might be saying:
1. God desired to create the universe
2. God thought or imagined the universe
3. God spoke the universe (uni-verse = Latin for ONE WORD)
4. His Creation appeared out of nothing

Everything proposed in this chapter is another in a long list of ongoing speculations concerning the origin and meaning of the mysterious Tetragrammaton. It is included in this study for the reader's consideration.

Isaiah 55:11
"So shall my word be that goeth forth out of my mouth: it shall not return unto me void, but it shall accomplish that which I please, and it shall prosper in the thing whereto I sent it."

Chapter 19

WRITTEN IN THE STARS

Psalms 19:1-14

"The heavens declare the glory of God; and the firmament shows His handiwork.

Day unto day utters speech, and night unto night reveals knowledge.

There is no speech nor language where their voice is not heard.

Their line has gone out through all the earth, and their words to the end of the world. In them He has set a tabernacle for the sun,

Which is like a bridegroom coming out of his chamber, and rejoices like a strong man to run its race.

Its rising is from one end of heaven, and its circuit to the other end; and there is nothing hidden from its heat.

The law of the LORD is perfect, converting the soul; the testimony of the LORD is sure, making wise the simple;

The statutes of the LORD are right, rejoicing the heart; the commandment of the LORD is pure, enlightening the eyes;

The fear of the LORD is clean, enduring forever; the judgments of the LORD are true and righteous altogether.

More to be desired are they than gold, yea, than much fine gold; sweeter also than honey and the honeycomb.

Moreover by them Your servant is warned, and in keeping them there is great reward.

Who can understand his errors? Cleanse me from secret faults.

Keep back Your servant also from presumptuous sins; let them not have dominion over me. Then I shall be blameless, and I shall be innocent of great transgression.

Let the words of my mouth and the meditation of my heart be acceptable in Your sight, O LORD, my strength and my Redeemer."

Some time ago I was listening to the radio and happened to hear a well known Bible teacher deliver a sermon on the real meaning of the Zodiac

Now, this subject has generated considerable interest and controversy for more than a century. One of the first books on the subject was *Mazzaroth — The Constellations*, by Miss Frances Rolleston and published in 1863. This was followed by E. W. Bullinger's book, *The Witness of the Stars*.

There have been many arguments against the theory that the Gospel is written by God in the night sky. However, so many coincidences exist on the matter that it is difficult to not give some credence to the idea. What follows is a condensation of the teaching from another point of view.

There are 12 signs of what has come to be known as the zodiac (meaning "Path") or the Mazzaroth (meaning "consecrated") as it is called in Job 38:32. They begin with Aries in the middle of March (around the time of the new moon) and finish in the middle of February with Pisces.

The prevailing views of those who have studied and written about the true meaning of the 12 signs (or "houses") of the zodiac and their companion stars, is that the signs begin with Virgo. This is a logical place for a Christian to place the first house since Jesus was born of a virgin, but it may not be correct. Furthermore, the sequence of the houses has a dramatic effect on their translation into the revealed plan of God.

First let me define the year in the Jewish economy. Rosh Hashana is the head of the year. This is the beginning of the civil year and it occurs in the Fall, September/October. In Exodus 12 God told Moses to begin the sacred year in the spring, March/April. So there are two types of years for the Jews: The civil year begins in the fall and the sacred year begins in the spring.

It just so happens that the sign of Virgo occurs at the time of Rosh Hashana, the Jewish civil new year. But, as we learn from Exodus 12:2, God instructed Moses that the sacred year, the year of the Feasts of the Lord, was to begin with the new moon of Nisan in the spring. I think it is no coincidence that Aries, the first sign of the zodiac, occurs in the spring with the beginning of the sacred the year.

The prevailing view (that the zodiac begins with Virgo) is based on the presumption that the Gospel begins with the virgin birth of Jesus. But I believe that the whole plan of God really begins with the Ram that Abraham took from the thicket on the summit of Moriah (which means "visions of God").

It can be shown that the new moon of March occurs precisely in the middle of the Jewish Civil Year. This symbolically places God in the middle of human affairs and begins His plan of salvation at the offering of Isaac by Abraham.

In the sign of Aries we can see the sacrificial Ram that God substituted for Abraham's sacrifice of his son Isaac. In the same way we can see in the Zodiac the promise of the coming of God's Son as our substitute.

We can see Jesus in the Ram of Genesis 22:13, right through to His return in Pisces as the Mighty King of the fishes. Between the Ram and the King, in the middle of the Zodiac, we find Virgo the Virgin.Can you see the relationship?

The Ram on Moriah as our substitution, the virgin birth of the Redeemer in Bethlehem, and the arrival of the King of the Universe at the end of the Church Age; three distinct and connected parts relating to both the Old and the New Testaments. Virgo is at the mid- point of the zodiac having five signs before her and six signs after her.

The first five signs are the types (the patterns of the promise). And the last six signs are the antitypes (the fulfillment of the promise). These correspond to the Old Testament shadows and the New Testament realities and between the two is the coming of Christ through virgin birth.

Now, there have been those who maintain that this just shows how Christianity is only a different slant on the pagan myths and legends of man's ignorant and superstitious past. But what they won't tell you is that this Mazzaroth predates the zodiac as the mystics have altered it by many centuries. In fact, its origin has been traced back to Enoch and it is entirely possible that God revealed it to man through Enoch before He translated him to heaven. (see Hebrews 11:5)

So the message in the stars was God's original revelation of the fulfillment of His promise to Adam and Eve at their fall. But Satan, the deceiver, perverted it into a device of prognostication, a philosophical machine and a mechanism for fortune-telling.

The real purpose of the zodiac is to reveal to all that God is in control of the destiny of man and that He keeps His word.

It is not my intention to present an in-depth study of the subject in this brief study. Rather I will continue with an exploded view of each of the Houses and how they relate to the Gospel of Christ. What follows is an overview of the 12 signs and some of their companion signs.

Aries: – The Chief is Found in Chapter 22 of Genesis as the Ram caught in the thicket. (The ancient Akkadians called it "Baraziggar" or "The sacrifice that makes right".)

Genesis 22:13
"And Abraham lifted up his eyes, and looked, and behold behind him a ram caught in a thicket by his horns: and Abraham went and took the ram, and offered him up for a burnt offering in the stead of his son."

Taurus: – The Bull (The beast of burden that was used in sacrifice.)

Psa 55:22 speaks of Christ is this way: *"Cast your burden on the Lord ...."* He is the Servant offered in sacrifice for many.

Gemini: – The Twins: Apollo and Hercules (This refers to the dual offices of Christ as King and Savior).

Isa 43:11

"I, even I, am the LORD; and beside me there is no saviour."

Cancer: – To hold fast and secure as in a crab's claw.

Rom 8:38-39

"For I am persuaded, that neither death, nor life, nor angels, nor principalities, nor powers, nor things present, nor things to come, nor height, nor depth, nor any other creature, shall be able to separate us from the love of God, which is in Christ Jesus our Lord."

Leo: – The Lion (Victory over the enemy and Lord of His domain.)

Col 2:15

"… having disarmed the powers and authorities, he made a public spectacle of them, triumphing over them by the cross."

Virgo: – The Virgin: The woman holding forth the Branch marks the coming of the Messiah and the beginning of the promised restoration.

Isa 4:2

"In that day the Branch of the LORD will be beautiful and glorious, and the fruit of the land will be the pride and glory of the survivors in Israel."

Libra: – The Scales (Man is tested). Man is out of balance without Christ.

Dan 5:27

"TEKEL; You are weighed in the balances, and are found wanting."

Scorpio: – Mortal Conflict. Its central star is Antares: "The wounding." A companion constellation is Ophiuchus: "the serpent holder." His left foot is being stung by the Scorpion but his right foot is on its head.

Gen 3:15

"And I will put enmity between you and the woman, And between your seed and her Seed; He shall bruise your head, And you shall bruise His heel."

Sagittarius: – The dual nature of Christ. Perfect in His humanity and perfect in His Deity. He is the archer whose arrow is aimed at the heart of the Scorpion.

Phil 2:5-7

"Let this mind be in you which was also in Christ Jesus, who, being in the form of God, did not consider it robbery to be equal with God, but made Himself of no reputation, taking the form of a bondservant, and coming in the likeness of men."

Capricorn: – The Sea Goat speaks of conversion. It is the goat becoming a fish. Transfiguration is God's purpose for those who love Him.

Rom 8:13

"For if you live according to the flesh you will die; but if by the Spirit you put to death the deeds of the body, you will live."

Aquarius: – The "Water Pourer." He is the giver of the Holy Spirit.

John 4:14
"... whoever drinks of the water that I shall give him will never thirst. But the water that I shall give him will become in him a fountain of water springing up into everlasting life."

Pisces: – The Fishes. The Egyptians knew it as "Pisces Hori": The fish of Him who comes. One of its stars is called in Hebrew, "Okda": The United. The fish are swimming in opposite directions but are connected to each other by a cord. This, I think, speaks of unity in diversity. It is interesting to note that while goats tend to do their own thing, fish travel in schools and move as one. The companion constellation is Cepheus: The King. Its Egyptian name is "Per-Ku-Hor" meaning "This One comes to rule."

Gen 1:16 tells us that God placed the stars in the heavens and Psalm 147:4 says that He named each one of them: "He counts the number of the stars; He calls them all by name."

Truly our God is a revealer and not a concealer. He has given us Special Revelation in the Holy Scriptures, and He has given us General Revelation in the heavens above us. Surely, *"Your Love O Lord reaches to the heavens."* **Psa 36:5**

Chapter 20

THE LIFE OF CHRIST

The "Word" Made Flesh

"In the beginning was the Word, and the Word was with God, and the Word was God. The same was in the beginning with God. All things were made by him; and without him was not any thing made that was made. In him was life; and the life was the light of men. And the light shineth in darkness; and the darkness comprehended it not.." **John 1:1-5**

Possibly nowhere else in all of literature has so much been said in so few words. From it we learn that the story of Jesus of Nazareth did not start with Gabriel's "annunciation" to Mary of the birth of the Messiah, but began in the throne room of God in eternity past with a Divine decree.

God, in His omniscience, foresaw the contamination of His creation by overt hostility toward Him. He therefore conceived a plan by which order would be restored in a way that would not compromise His character or integrity. God decreed that at the appointed time He would clothe Himself in flesh and blood, willingly subjecting Himself to the limitations of the flesh, and present Himself to man as a man.

It is only by knowing Christ Jesus of Nazareth, that we can know God personally. Jesus said, in John 10:30, "I and my Father are one." Without Jesus (His personality, His character, His attitudes and viewpoints) God remains abstract and is essentially a three-letter word that evokes an ambivalent response of fear, obsequiousness, respect and resentment.

In his book, *To Know Christ Jesus*, author F. J. Sheed says, *"The truth 'Christ is God' is a statement not only about Christ but about God. Without it we could still know of God, certainly, but in His own nature only; infinite, omnipotent, creating of nothing, sustaining creation in being. [However] it would be a remote kind of knowledge, for of none of these ways of being or doing have we any personal experience. In Christ Jesus we can see God in our nature, experiencing the things we have experienced, coping with situations we have to cope with. Thereby we know God [in a way that] the most devout pagan cannot know Him."[9]*

From this it becomes obvious that a sound knowledge of Jesus and His teachings is absolutely essential to a personal relationship with God the Father. In John 14:6 Jesus assures us that no one comes to the Father except through Him.

One thing that would seem to be true of all spirit-filled Christians is that they are always hungry for knowledge about Jesus and His teachings. If we do not know Him as a man in His incarnation, we are in danger of constructing a Christ out of our own imagination or needs. If we remove Him from history He becomes nothing more than a principle or idea that stimulates the intellect and justifies a moral ideal.

---

9 To Know Christ Jesus by F.J.Sheed c1962 Sheed and Ward Ltd. London. Page xv of the Forward.

In John 8:31-32 Jesus said, *"... If ye continue in my word, then are ye my disciples indeed; And ye shall know the truth, and the truth shall make you free."*

We must learn and obey His word and put our trust in Him, and not in spiritual experiences or unbiblical faith.

In John 14:20, He said that He is in the Father and that we are in Him. At the sealing of the new covenant, men were to be united with the divine nature. But without knowing Jesus the Christ and obeying His teachings can we be truly redeemed?

The Incarnation

About 400 years after the last of the Old Testament prophets, the "Son" of the Living God was conceived of human flesh. Perhaps this occurred on the anniversary of the "Pax Romana" or "Peace of Rome". (That was the day that Augustus Caesar closed the doors of the temple of Janus located in the Forum - January 13th)

The birth of the Messiah had been prophesied throughout the Old Testament and was finally announced to an astonished Mary by no less than the angel Gabriel. Gabriel also told her that Elizabeth, her relative, was already six months pregnant with the witness who would prepare the people for the ministry of the Christ.

The night of Jesus' birth was unique in all of history. Some extra Canonical sources tell us that while He was being born, the skies over Bethlehem and the surrounding hills were filled with light and the sounds of heavenly voices and music. Whether that is true or not it is without doubt that the night of Jesus' birth was unique in all of human history.

Shepherds, people belonging to a profession considered to be beneath all but the lowest levels of society, were invited by angels to bear witness to the birth of the Messiah in a cave reserved for domestic animals. The Christ came to earth in a way that made Him available to all people regardless of their social or economic or political standing.

From the moment that the Christ entered the realm of the "enemy", the forces of darkness were hard at work to terminate God's plan of redemption. The treacherous king Herod was a willing tool of those forces when he ordered the death of all the infants less than two years of age in Bethlehem, in an insane attempt to protect his royal position. He had hoped that by such a strategic slaughter, he would surely eliminate the Jew that prophecy, he feared, made heir to his throne.

But Divine providence saw to it that the infant would escape Herod's will. In a dream (or was it a vision?) Joseph was warned of the disaster and told to take the child and His mother to safety in Egypt. Some time after this flight, Herod died from a rare and terrible disease and so they returned to Nazareth.

From this time until Jesus began His public ministry, the Gospels tell us of only one incident involving the young Jesus. At about the age of 12, Jesus accompanied His parents to Jerusalem for the Passover celebration.

After the celebration, He became separated from His parents and, after searching for Him for three days, they found Him amazing the doctors and teachers with His depth of understanding of the law. Of the next 18 years of Jesus' life, the Gospels tell us only that He "grew in wisdom and stature and in favor with God and men." (Luke 2:52)

Meanwhile, Elizabeth's son, John (a prophet of priestly descent), was living an ascetic life in the wilderness in preparation of giving his testimony confirming the deity of Jesus of Nazareth in accordance with prophecy. In convicting his generation of sin and calling for repentance, John the Baptist made many enemies in high places; a fact that assured him of a martyr's death at the hands of Herod's son, Antipas, shortly after Jesus began His public ministry.

At the foreordained time, Jesus appeared to John from among a crowd of people who were seeking ceremonial ablution at the hands of the prophet. John immediately recognized Jesus as the Messiah and, although feeling inadequate, baptized Him so that the prophecy might be fulfilled. At this time, a voice from heaven was pleased to declare Jesus as His Son (In 2Pet. 1:16-18 we find reason to think that this voice may have been heard by many at that gathering).

After receiving the baptism, Jesus went off into the wilderness to prepare Himself for the tasks that lay ahead of Him. During these 40 days, Jesus was tempted three times by Satan to abort His mission. On each of these occasions Jesus silenced Satan quickly with a simple declaration of scripture.

Some time after breaking His fast, Jesus began to gather together a small band of disciples whom He had been given by the Father to accompany Him throughout His ministry and continue His ministry after His ascension.

Jesus reluctantly performed His first miracle while He and His disciples were attending a wedding in Cana, which is located in Galilee. Before the wedding was over, all the wine was consumed, and Mary asked her son Jesus to replenish it. Jesus explained that the time for Him to begin performing miracles in public had not yet arrived but, in true filial love, He honored His mother's wish and, with the knowledge of only His mother and a few of the servants, turned common water into the finest wine. Soon after this Jesus left for Galilee.

On the way He had to go through Samaria, where He met a Samaritan woman drawing water from a well that had belonged to the Jacob of the Genesis account. Jesus convinced her that He was the Messiah, and because of her testimony many Samaritans were converted.

Jesus continued on His journey to Galilee and, once more at Cana, He met a royal official who begged Him to heal his son, who was near death in Capernaum, of a fatal sickness.

Herod imprisoned John the Baptist and when Jesus heard of this, He went and lived in Capernaum to fulfill what was prophesied by the prophet Isaiah.

Jesus began to preach the kingdom of heaven and was received well everywhere but in Nazareth, where He was rejected because they thought that they already knew who He was from the years He had spent there during His childhood. (In John 4:44 Jesus tells us that a prophet is without honor in his own country.)

The people of Nazareth attempted to kill Jesus but, since it was not time for His death, He walked right through the crowd and went His way.

One day at the Sea of Galilee, Jesus boarded a boat belonging to Simon Peter and asked him to take Him away from the shore a little so that He could teach the people gathered there from the boat. Jesus then instructed the fishermen to once more, after an unsuccessful night of fishing, let down their nets. With mild protests the fishermen did as Jesus said and were amazed to catch as many fish as their nets could hold.

After a demonstration of such authority over nature, the fishermen accepted Jesus' invitation to follow Him and become fishers of men. Thus were added to the little band of close disciples Simon, Andrew, James, and John.

Jesus continued preaching and healing and casting out unclean spirits throughout Galilee and began to feel the opposition of the authorities.

Once more teaching at Galilee, Jesus met a tax collector named Matthew and added him to His small group of special disciples. Then Jesus attended a great banquet at Matthew's house where He shared the company of tax collectors and many others who were considered "sinners" by the Pharisees and the teachers of the law. These authorities brought many scathing criticisms against Jesus and His disciples as a result of Jesus' disregard of their cherished conventions, including fasting and Sabbath restrictions.

Jesus continued healing and preaching the kingdom of heaven, and one day, after a night of praying on a mountainside near the sea of Galilee, Jesus designated, from among all of His disciples, twelve who were to receive special training and become His apostles.

These twelve were: Simon Peter, his brother Andrew, James, John, Philip, Bartholomew, Matthew, Thomas, James son of Alphaeus, Simon who was called the Zealot, Judas son of James, and Judas Iscariot, who was to one day betray Him.

Then Jesus and His disciples went down to a level place and saw a great number of people from all over Judea and Jerusalem, and the coast of Tyre and Sidon, who had come to learn from Him and be healed of their diseases. Many were healed by the power that was coming from Him.

With so many people to hear Him, Jesus went up on a mountainside and began to teach them. Many consider this "Sermon on the Mount" to be the most familiar and instructive sermon ever presented by Jesus. It embodies the essence of Christian doctrine and represents the teaching half of the two-fold purpose of the incarnation; the other was expiation or atonement.

Jesus continued to teach by parable and example and to perform miracles and do other things which, as the apostle John said in the conclusion of his Gospel, were so numerous that "if they were written one by one, I suppose that even the world itself could not contain the books that would be written." (John 21:25)

Through all, Jesus demonstrated enormous capacity for understanding and caring even for those who, in their ignorance, caused Him to suffer.

As Jesus continued with His Father's work throughout the land, an enraged and indignant Jewish hierarchy was plotting His end. The powers of darkness were unwittingly helping the Divine plan to achieve God's purpose.

In about the third year of His public ministry, just before the Jewish Passover, Jesus went to Jerusalem and found merchants in the temple courts selling goods and exchanging money (the temple had its own currency) for a price.

Jesus, in an uncharacteristic rage, drove them from the temple. When they asked for a sign that would prove that He had the authority to make changes to such a profitable tradition, Jesus told them, "Destroy this temple, and I will raise it again in three days." (Jn 2:13-19) Naturally, since they did not know that Jesus was speaking of His own body and its resurrection from death, they scoffed and mocked Him.

While Jesus was in Jerusalem during that Passover feast, the stage was set and the curtain was rising on the final act of the drama that "the whole of creation" groaned in anticipation of. (Romans 8:21-22) The lamb of expiation had presented Himself to His slayers.

So celebrated was His entry into Jerusalem on that "Palm Sunday," that even His apostles thought that Jesus was to become the king of Israel. They were so sure of this, in fact, that they began to speculate on what positions each of them may receive in the new government.

On a Wednesday evening in a place referred to as "the upper room", Jesus celebrated the last Passover of His ministry with His apostles. During this meal Jesus instituted the most important ordinance in the Christian church: The memorial of the Lord's

Supper (a teaching ceremony to remind believers of how it is just as important for the soul to receive nourishment through the Word of God as it is for the body to receive nourishment through physical food).

Meanwhile, the rulers of the Jews were bringing together the final details of the intricate conspiracy that would result in the ignominious death of the only wholly righteous human being ever to breathe the air of planet earth. His only crime was challenging the cherished traditions of men that oppose the righteousness of God.

Tradition tells us that Rome, through Pontius Pilate, disdainfully distanced itself from Jewish internal affairs thus seeming to attach its approval to the persecution and execution of Jesus of Nazareth. However, respected historians have left records to show that in that day and age, Rome was renowned throughout the world for its justice and honor. But not even the might and justice of Rome could save the Lamb of expiation and stop God's saving plan from succeeding.

There is so much passion electrifying the arrest, trial and crucifixion of Jesus, that it is easy to lose sight of the Divine hand orchestrating the complex details of the whole event. It was meant to happen. It was God's will. No power on earth could stop it. Thank God.

From Wimps To Conquerors

Three days after the crucifixion of Jesus of Nazareth, the little band of His followers, shaken and confused, were huddled in a room behind locked doors. They were desperately considering the news that they had recently received from the women who went to the tomb in order to prepare the body of Jesus. The women had told them that Jesus had risen from the dead and Mary Magdalene said that He had appeared to her just outside the tomb that morning.

These men could hardly believe what they were hearing. At first this resistance to the testimony of the women may seem strange in view of the fact that these were the same men who had lived with Jesus and learned from Him. They had heard Him announce, at a time when it seemed that everything was going their way, that He would soon be killed and then rise up from the grave.

However, it must be remembered that their expectation of a Jewish Messiah was no different than the commonly held idea that He would be a conquering king who would rally the people of Israel against the Roman intruders and drive them back to Rome.

The disciples were Jews and as such their thinking was strongly nationalistic. They had completely missed the universality of the Messiah and in true Jewish fashion considered Him the property of Israel. When He died on the cross, all their hopes of a Jewish conquest died with Him.

Now there was a new development; this Jesus was something special after all. Did they dare to hope that the women were right? If Jesus had risen from the dead then certainly they needed to re-evaluate their opinions of Him. Quite likely at this point they still harbored the hope that He would drive the Romans from their land and establish His kingdom with His disciples appointed as His executives.

At any rate, Jesus was suddenly in the room with them, regardless of the locked doors, and all the conjecture abruptly gave way to wonder and excitement mixed with relief.

Jesus continued to instruct His disciples until His ascension at which time He told them to wait in Jerusalem and expect to receive power from God to spread the good news.

The disciples had already been given the "great commission" to spread the Gospel, but did not really get started until after the Spirit of God had empowered them 49 days later at the feast of Pentecost just as Christ had promised.

In modern terms, before their endorsement by the Holy Spirit in Jerusalem, the disciples were wimps. Following the Pentecost incidence, we can see a miraculous transformation; the disciples had become the Apostles (ambassadors, divinely commissioned by Christ Himself)

They were now confident, courageous men, energetically broadcasting the seeds of Christianity by passionately proclaiming the Gospel to a people desperate for liberation from a hopeless and meaningless existence.

The Human Condition

Henry David Thoreau, the noted essayist and poet of the mid 19th century, set forth a profound observation when he wrote, "The mass of men lead lives of quiet desperation."

Man is desperately reaching for a self-reliance that he will never achieve. We are prone to think that we are standing on the threshold of a "golden age". But this optimism is limited to those of us who are enjoying good health and far enough away from our foreseeable demise so that we are able to avoid thinking about it.

The fact is that most of us don't start to give our pathetic condition much thought until old age, or ill health, or the death of a loved one intrudes into our carefully cultivated apathy. Perhaps you've learned how very easy it is to deceive ourselves that we are brave while there is nothing to be brave about. And it's quite simple to cope with suffering, as long as it's academic.

When the time comes (and it always does) to be checked out on our bravery or toughness quotient, we are almost always disappointed with what we find out about ourselves. The more fortunate persons among us discover at an early age that humans are inherently weak. No matter how strong or how smart we are, we all end up in the same condition: Third grade fertilizer.

So far I have painted a rather dismal picture of human life on the individual level. For the person who does not believe in God however, it is an accurate picture. Any hope he may have of continuing to exist vicariously through his works or his children are just another type of illusion. Few individuals can feel completely comfortable with the prospect of their mortality and a resignation to extinction. It just is not normal.

The really strange part of all of this is that such people will smugly reject what they consider to be a Christian illusion without realizing that what they have chosen to accept in its place is itself an illusion and, when subjected to the same demands for proof that are imposed on the Christian world view, will collapse just as quickly.

Christianity, however, is not an illusion. Two thousand years ago a unique and wonderful person suffered a life of self-imposed restriction so that each one of us would have hope and could know the answers to life's most difficult questions.

Faith

Some people seem to be quite content to accept another's experience as if it had real personal value to them whereas, many find that there is absolutely nothing to be gained by such second-hand experiences. But in fact, we all rely heavily on the efforts of those who precede us.

It's nice to think that we keep coming up with all sorts of new ideas, but in reality there is probably very little (outside of science and technology) that has not already been thought of and experienced by others. We are continually discovering and rediscovering and rearranging the thoughts and ideas of countless thousands of people who have been here before us. So no matter how we look at it, we are all affected by the experiences of others.

We are raised in a system that teaches us to demand proof before acceptance. This is sufficient in most cases but is quite inappropriate when it comes to "religion" which, by nature, is resistant to proof and objective analysis. Revelation, not experience, is the fuel of religious conversion.

At this point it becomes appropriate to define faith. Hebrews 11:1 tells us that "faith is the substance of things hoped for, the evidence of things not seen." Some Christians interpret this to mean belief without knowledge, or "blind" faith.

The more knowledgeable are convinced that it is some mysterious force or "substance" given to the believer by God to enable him to accept salvation. Those in the New Age movement speculate that it is some magical energy that will give them power to carry out their will.

A word study of the definition given in Heb 11:1 will show that none of the above are correct. What God is telling us in Hebrews 11:1 is that faith is a conviction of the truth of something based on knowledge that results in the willingness to operate assumptively. This in turn confirms or assures the reality of the things assumed and validates our faith.

It can be seen from this that faith is not the exclusive property of religion; it is applied in the secular world daily. For example, if you want a room added to your house, you "contract" a tradesman for that purpose. This contract is an understanding of what the tradesman will do, and what you will pay him for doing it. You then pay a deposit to get the job started. This deposit is an expression of your faith that the job will be done.

Faith as applied to God is only different from this example in that we do not experience Him in the same way as we do the tradesman. Also if the tradesman defaults, society provides a way by which we may be able to hold him accountable. However, if God defaults (and He never will), there is no higher authority to go to.

As a result it becomes necessary to know the terms of the agreement with God and to trust Him. This trust must come from a clear knowledge of the nature and character of God which can only be obtained from a strong familiarity with His Word.

Many of us find ourselves far too busy paying attention to all the "practical" things of life to have any time for spiritual matters. And yet most of us are living "lives of quiet desperation". We think that sooner or later the desperation will leave if we just hang in there.

Some of us seek the aid of psychologists. If you have been addressing your "desperation" in any way other than through Christ, then it is unlikely that you have achieved any **lasting** success. Genuine peace and happiness are achievable to anybody willing to go after them with the same energy that most people apply to the pursuit of business or pleasure.

Your efforts will, however, be in vain if you look in the wrong place; such is a misapplication of faith. It should be remembered that faith is only as good as the object of said faith; and the only reliable object of faith is Christ.

Christianity cannot be proven. However, the evidence in support of it is overwhelming. Again, demand proof of any other world view and subject it to the same scrutiny and you will soon see how poorly it measures up.

It is assumed by many that Christianity is only a deception and that it preys on the weak or mentally deficient. This is not only insulting but shows an astounding ignorance of the subject. Some of the intellectual giants of humanity have been the strongest believers of God and His Word.

Historical Christ

Since it is claimed that Jesus of Nazareth is the answer to man's desperation, the reality of His existence and His genuineness is of paramount importance. Here I will endeavor to show that Jesus was a real person and that He was what He claimed to be. The reader is entitled only to reasonable proof, so must be content with the same criteria that he or she accepts regarding any other personage who lived so long ago - such as Alexander the Great or Julius Caesar or Josephus.

The historical existence of Jesus has already been established to the satisfaction of historians and others who have been willing to accept the evidence. In addition to the Christian writings, there are records concerning Jesus in existence today that were written by His enemies as well as by disinterested parties.

To say that all these records were the result of a gigantic and well organized hoax is to say that we must subject all historical data to impossibly stringent scrutiny.

Jesus of Nazareth claimed to be the son of God. More than that, He said that He and His Father were one and the same. He said that in the Son, we see the Father and that He had been given a divine destiny for the benefit of all those people who would accept Him.

He told us that we have souls and spirits in addition to our bodies. He said that we would be presented with many gods and many explanations of the meaning of life, but that He alone was the truth. Then He went about performing miracles to show that He had the authority to back up everything He said.

Jesus didn't only heal people and feed people and raise people from the dead, but in calming a storm on the sea of Galilee, He also manipulated the elements; so much for slight of hand.

There have been gurus and avatars, prophets and philosophers from the beginning of history, but this Jesus is unique in that He is the only person ever to claim to be one with God. Was He lying? Was He insane? Was He telling us the truth?

Jesus would have to have been the ultimate hypocrite if He was lying; yet His life was free of any evidence of hypocrisy. A study of the records will satisfy anyone who wishes to substantiate this.

There is a beautiful consistency awaiting the sincere and persistent explorer as he searches the demeanor and teachings of Jesus of Nazareth which will convince him that insanity is out of the question. This includes delusion. Nobody else in history has successfully deluded the elements.

Was it His purpose to lead the Jews to freedom from the Romans and to have Himself set up and worshiped as the king of the nation of Israel? Certainly the Jews thought that to be true; and when they found out that they had assumed wrongly, in their great disappointment they had Him executed.

Or was it His intention that a new and different organization be set up so that a group of elitists (priests) could extort the best of food and material goods from a superstitious and fearful Gentile public? Not likely in view of the fact that by declaring that every believer is a priest Jesus actually put an entire profession out of work; professional priests are without scriptural endorsement.

The function of the priest was always to present the people's petition to God through the performance of rituals (many of which were quite complex and took a great deal of training to perform properly). Jesus eliminated the need for this "middle man" when He declared that all believers were priests and as such had personal access to God through prayer. The believer must receive teaching in order to mature in the faith; therefore the legitimate position of pastor/teacher replaced the priesthood in the early Christian church.

I have shown how we can reasonably accept, at least as a working hypothesis, the reality of the historical and Divine Jesus. I submit that any attempt to prove that Jesus is just a pretty story made up by some well-meaning group will be met with even more difficulty than attempting to prove Him real.

A close look at history will reveal that Jesus of Nazareth is the only person ever to have died and lived again, in the same body, a few days after his death (a denial, at the very least by example, of the counterfeit teaching of reincarnation).

His death and subsequent resurrection were witnessed by a very large number of people and, historians generally agree, remains one of the best documented events of the ancient world.

The controversy surrounding the resurrection of Jesus is not unique to our present "enlightened age", but was in full bloom while many of the witnesses to the event were still alive. However, unlike modern contention, this controversy did not always involve a denial that the resurrection did in fact occur (many of Christ's enemies had to concede to that). Their purpose was to obscure its meaning. But we are told by Jesus Himself what it all means.

So, are we to look to the persuasive arguments of a few deep thinkers such as Confucius, Buddha, Plato, Freud, Nietzsche, Maharishi Mahesh Yogi, or Timothy Leary to give an understanding of life that it is beyond our human abilities to explore?

The resurrection and ascension of Jesus as attested to by hundreds of witnesses, is the culmination of a life lived in proof of the qualifications of the only man ever to speak with authority on the purpose of life. To follow the teachings of any other is to follow the blind into a quagmire of confusion, delusion, and despair.

Jesus knew that without His witness to the real nature and purpose of reality, man would be the victim of endless theories and ideas, each leading farther from the truth. While it is true that the "mass of men" does still rely heavily on such vain philosophizing, thanks to the God/man Jesus, it is now a matter of choice rather than an inevitable consequence of our sentient nature.

Finally, the author of the famous Ontological argument for the existence of God, Anselm of Canterbury, contended that faith precedes reason and that reason can expand faith. He is responsible for the profound statement, *"I do not seek to understand that I may believe, but I believe that I may understand; for this I know, that unless I first believe, I shall not understand."*

So I invite you, dear reader, to put aside any bias you might have against Christ and submit to Him for a month. Qualify yourself to judge the veracity of the Biblical record by reading the Gospels for yourself. Then put Him to the test. What is one month out of your life? You stand to gain more than you can imagine if you just give it a try.

Jesus has promised life in greater measure to any who will trust His as Savior.

John 10:10
"… I am come that they might have life, and that they might have it more abundantly."

Jesus said, *"Come unto me, all ye that labour and are heavy laden, and I will give you rest. Take my yoke upon you, and learn of me; for I am meek and lowly in heart: and ye shall find rest unto your souls. For my yoke is easy, and my burden is light."* **Matt 11:28-30**

Chapter 21

EPILOGUE

THE PLAN
(A possible Genesis as imagined by the author)

"And we have known and believed the love that God hath to us. God is love; and he that dwelleth in love dwelleth in God, and God in him." **1 John 4:16**

Every story has a beginning. And the story of Creation starts in eternity past. What follows is a dramatized overview of Creation based on what has been revealed in the Scriptures.

Once upon eternity, in a place called the most high, LOVE felt within Himself a great stirring. With a rush of pure joy His very thoughts cascaded into the space that was expanding around Him. He smiled. He had whispered the universe into existence. Its myriad suns and clusters and gases were all wonderful manifestations of His Divine Mind. His plan had begun.

As He continued to brood over His marvelous creation, He felt another stirring within His nature. Out from His very essence there shimmered into existence a complex matrix of self-awareness. This "angel" was followed quickly by another, and yet another, and another; until there were vast multitudes of them.

These angels, had no need to be told who they were or what their purpose was; each had been created with a name and all the knowledge they needed. They knew that it is the very nature of LOVE to create and nurture.

He provided for their every need so that they were free to enjoy pure existence. An eternity of delight and discovery awaited them within this infinite Kingdom. They were unencumbered by any cares, for all their needs were provided by their Creator.

LOVE cherished His creation. But He knew that His offspring carried within themselves the capacity to corrupt their universe. Yes, there were rough times ahead for His creatures. But He would lovingly guide them to an eternal and perfect maturity.

For a very long time the universe was alive with the activity of angelic beings praising their Creator and enjoying their community. But the time came, as LOVE knew it would, when His angels discovered that they had the ability to make choices. The first to make this discovery was a very beautiful cherub named Lucifer, and he became very excited at this new dimension to his life.

Lucifer learned that he was no longer confined to the nature that LOVE had given him at creation. Just as any baby begins to explore and soon discovers something new, Lucifer discovered attitudes and ideas that were different from those of his Creator; some even opposing His Holy will.

As Lucifer experimented, he became increasingly resentful of his Creator and thought of Him as unfair. Eventually he was overwhelmed by a consuming arrogance; the very opposite of LOVE's gracious nature. LOVE tried to teach him how to use his power of choice properly, but Lucifer's response was only a stubborn resistance. He became hostile to his Creator and sought to destroy His great plan. Lucifer had introduced wickedness into the universe and the consequences that follow were sure to be disastrous.

While Lucifer was encouraging the malignant changes that were corrupting his being, the rest of the angelic host were watching with great interest. LOVE compassionately tried to guide Lucifer to a full understanding of what was happening to him. But the implacable Lucifer did not trust his Creator to know what was best.

In a burst of enormous conceit, He accused LOVE of unfairness and abuse of power. This shocked the angelic host. He also accused LOVE of predestining rebellion in him by giving him free will. This slanderous folly immediately catapulted Lucifer forever out of the loving reach of the Creator. He had become Satan, the accuser.

These accusations did not go unnoticed by the angelic host and a third of them agreed with Satan. In so doing they joined themselves to him in opposing LOVE. The remaining two thirds of the angels continued their allegiance to the Creator although many of them were not sure that there wasn't some merit to Satan's allegations. The universe had become polluted. Satan's rebellion had brought about division in the Kingdom and had infected the universe with decay.

Aware that the angelic host were confused and disturbed by Satan's charges, LOVE initiated the second phase of His plan. He focused His attention on the earth where He created a garden that was insulated from the corruption of the surrounding universe.

Within this garden He took the elements of the earth and molded from them a new creature in His own likeness. And when He had completed the form, He breathed awareness into it and it became Adam.

And so began mankind, whose wonderful destiny it was to vindicate LOVE's righteousness and be joined with Him through His Holy Spirit. But Satan, fearful of the Divine Plan, took advantage of Adam's innocence and infected him with rebellion. So Adam had to leave the delights of LOVE's perfect garden and live in the corruption of the world outside.

But even as Adam entered his curse, LOVE declared a promise. One would come, from the seed of the woman, who would deliver Adam's sons from the rule of the Devil. He would crush the head of the Serpent and resolve the angelic conflict. He would restore unity to the Kingdom.

For unto us a child is born, unto us a son is given: and the government shall be upon his shoulder: and his name shall be called Wonderful, Counsellor, The mighty God, The everlasting Father, The Prince of Peace. **Isaiah 9:6**

Bibliography

All Scripture from King James Version of the Bible.

Kolatch, Alfred J. *The Jewish Book Of Why*. New York: Jonathan David Publishers, Inc., 1981.

Version 2.5. *Merriam-Webster's Collegiate Dictionary*. Dallas, Tx: Zane Publishing, Inc., 1994-96.

Jones, Alfred. *Jones' Dictionary Of Old Testament Proper Names*. Michigan: Kregel Publications, 1990.

James Gilbertson. *PC Study Bible For Windows*. Seattle, WA: Biblesoft, 1998.

Morris, Henry. *The Biblical Basis For Modern Science*. Grand Rapids, Mi: Baker Book House, 1984.

About the Author

David Puffer Th.B., is from Brisbane, Australia. He has served as pastor and worship leader in several churches as well as teaching on a radio program called "The Exousia Experience."

After 30 years of diligent study of the Scriptures, David is anxious to share his discoveries with other truth seekers. He and his wife Camellia live and serve in Pittsburgh, Pa.

More information can be found on their website: www.exousia. org.